NIGHTMARE
ON THE
SCOTTIE

NIGHTMARE
ON THE
SCOTTIE

THE MAIDEN VOYAGE OF A
DOOMED KING CRABBER

STEPHEN D. ORSINI

BASALT BOOKS

Basalt Books
PO Box 645910
Pullman, Washington 99164-5910
Phone: 800-354-7360
Email: basalt.books@wsu.edu
Website: basaltbooks.wsu.edu

Library of Congress Cataloging-in-Publication Data

Names: Orsini, Stephen D., 1948- author.
Title: Nightmare on the Scottie : the maiden voyage of a doomed king
    crabber / [Stephen D. Orsini].
Description: Pullman, Washington : Basalt Books, [2022] | Includes
    bibliographical references.
Identifiers: LCCN 2022007624 | ISBN 9781638640004 (Paperback)
Subjects: LCSH: Orsini, Stephen D., 1948---Travel. | Seafaring life. |
    Scottie (Boat) | Ship trials. | Severe storms--Panama Canal (Panama) |
    Survival at sea. | College students--United States. | Coming of
    age--United States.
Classification: LCC G530.O77 A3 2022 | DDC 910.4/5--dc23/eng/20220404
LC record available at https://lccn.loc.gov/2022007624

Basalt Books is an imprint of Washington State University Press.
The Washington State University Pullman campus is located on the homelands of the
Niimíipuu (Nez Perce) Tribe and the Palus people. We acknowledge their presence
here since time immemorial and recognize their continuing connection to the land, to
the water, and to their ancestors. WSU Press is committed to publishing works that
foster a deeper understanding of the Pacific Northwest and the contributions of its
Native peoples.

Cover design by Hannah Gaskamp.
Cover photo by Matt Hardy

CONTENTS

To Anne McCracken
for passing on her unflagging dedication to literature,
the arts, and the life of the mind.

INTRODUCTION

Nightmare on the Scottie is a true sea story unique to the Pacific Northwest, a consequence of the rapid development of the Alaskan King Crab fishery. By December 1969, this lucrative fishery had become, like Klondike gold and North Slope oil, another Alaskan "gold rush." Those early in reaped huge profits. Stories circulated of skippers paying off their new king crab boats in a season. Alaskan king crab legs became the "hot" item on seafood menus across the country.

Because Alaska king crab migrate from deeper waters to the continental shelf of the Bering Sea starting in December, fishing, with 700-pound pots made of steel rebar, is conducted in winter in some of the most dangerous waters in the world in freezing, sub-arctic darkness. (The challenges of this winter fishery became legend in the popular Discovery Channel series *The Deadliest Catch* which in its third season garnered 49 million viewers.)

Corporate interests involved in the fishing industry wanted in, but Pacific Northwest shipyards, like Seattle's Marco Marine, were plugged with orders for new king crabbers. One of these corporations, Westgate, contracted with Bender Shipyard in Mobile, Alabama, to build two king crab vessels for the Alaskan fishery. Bender Shipyard built shrimpers and oil rig supply boats mainly for the Gulf of Mexico, but had no experience building vessels for the rigors of a winter fishery in the Bering Sea. Nevertheless, Bender wanted in on this booming vessel market. Meanwhile, Westgate was

The crew on the *Scottie*'s maiden voyage: Steve, left, and Jack.

pushing to have its new vessels in Dutch Harbor, Alaska, the epicenter of the new king crab industry, for the 1970 season.

The sea and commercial fishing have been a way of life for coastal communities of Washington and Oregon since their founding. The richness and diversity of Alaskan fisheries remain economic drivers in communities like the Ballard neighborhood in Seattle and Anacortes, Washington. Growing up in the Pacific Northwest, certain young men and women from such communities yearned to go to sea on a commercial fishing boat.

One of the two Westgate vessels, the *Scottie*, was ready for delivery in December 1969. Westgate needed a delivery crew to bring the vessel from the Mobile shipyard via the Panama Canal to Seattle for final outfitting. Two college students, both involved in the Pacific Northwest fishing industry in summers, heard that two deck hands were needed in addition to the already hired captain and engineer to round out the delivery crew. With a long Christmas break, the two signed on for the delivery voyage. They envisioned steaming through sun-drenched waters of the Caribbean and transiting the Panama Canal to arrive on the West Coast in time to resume January classes. Instead, *Scottie* steamed into a major late-season Caribbean storm with high winds and seas that battered the new vessel and her crew all the way to the Panama Canal. Many of the inadequately tested systems in the vessel failed. After days of mounting seas, *Scottie* nearly capsized when hit by a huge rogue wave.

Nightmare on the Scottie is a coming-of-age sea story for the two young men. What started as a winter escape from the long shadow of the Vietnam war clouding their senior year became a life-threatening event. In addition to equipment failure, human frailties compounded the danger. The two survived the voyage, wiser in the realities of the nautical world. As in Joseph Conrad's sea story *Youth*, the "romance of illusion" propelled them into an event they would value all their lives.

CHAPTER I
THE VERITABLE QUANDARY

By all that's wonderful it is the sea, I believe, the sea itself—or is it youth alone? Who can tell? But you here—you all had something out of life: money, love—whatever one gets on shore—and, tell me, wasn't that the best time, that time when we were young at sea; young and had nothing, on the sea that gives nothing, except hard knocks—and sometimes a chance to feel your strength—that only—what you all regret?

—Joseph Conrad, *Youth*

The din of Portland, Oregon's Southwest Madison Street traffic diminished a decibel or two as I turned the corner onto First Street. A sharp southerly gust swirled around the parking structure on my right driving the rain into my face. No other pedestrian braved the stormy night.

On the east side of First, a blue awning protruded over the sidewalk. The awning clung to a narrow building fronting on First but extending nearly a full block toward the Willamette River. The brick structure—my destination—was an anachronism amongst its more modern neighbors, dating from the era when the river thrived as the central artery of trade and transport.

Reaching the protective awning, I stood for a long moment trying to remember when I had last visited the Veritable Quandary to quaff a brew and ponder the philosophies of the day. I entered and to my delight found her still there, her skin creamy pale white, her arms open and welcoming above small bare breasts. She hung high on the brick wall, her eyes on the horizon. The essence of the lost art of the figurehead, she once adorned the

1

prow of a sailing ship. She represented a sailor's fancy, but not the painted damsel of the shore. No gaudy clothes or make-up; with her black hair pulled tightly back, she embodied the spirit of seafaring, of the long journey across the purifying sea.

The Veritable Quandary had become a haunting symbol of roads not taken. Many years earlier, my friend Jack[1] and I had conceived of starting such an establishment late one night. We even spent afternoons looking at potential venues. Undercapitalized, we eventually were forced to exchange the publican dream for attainable professions. Jack would agree with me now that we had overestimated those professions. I wondered, standing in the entry, if Jack, the busy attorney, would even show up for this reunion.

As I walked toward the back of the long narrow bar, I saw him at a dimly lit table. Twenty years had not bloated his features. He stood to greet me with a handshake, and his physique was still that of a young man. Although his skin had not wrinkled, it was tighter: the lips, never generous, were thinner. His smile no longer had the ease of youth but was the taut grimace of the attorney, witness to all the vagaries of human interaction. The bags under his eyes showed the years of the tyranny of small print.

In that instant of scrutiny, of the handshake, I wondered what Jack saw. He had become an attorney. Even with all the nefarious associations, at least it was a profession. Indecision had shaped my career. The ebb and flow of events, unfulfilled dreams, love, and children had landed me in a salesman's job peddling large commercial power-generation equipment. No doubt he saw the graying hair at my temples. I weighed the same as when I walked forward to collect my bachelor of arts diploma, but the lines of crow's feet now framed my eyes. Beyond these exterior markings, I wondered if he could discern the miles of travel, the endless hotel rooms, and the thousands of frustrating meetings.

"How's the world treating you?" I asked in the discomfort of old friends grown apart.

"The world does not treat," he said.

"Touché," I said, slightly embarrassed.

As we sat down, the waitress arrived.

"What can I get for you?" she asked. She placed two napkins down, one in

---

1 Although this is a work of nonfiction, some names have been changed to protect the privacy of the individuals.

front of each of us. As she leaned forward, her rich brown hair tumbled over her shoulder. When she stood up, she tossed it back with a flick of her head. Her eyes were large and strikingly blue. She gave off a delicate scent and had the clear complexion of Northwestern girls who eschew make-up. Hers was the promise of feminine warmth, the allure of youthful sensuality. All this Jack absorbed in a sidelong glance that I caught from the corner of my eye.

"A bourbon and seven," said the attorney.

"I'll take a Heineken," said the salesman.

She turned and walked away, leaving us to ourselves.

"Wasn't it your fault?" Jack asked with the hint of a smile.

"I could hardly take all the credit. I recall a joint plot hatched over Tillamook cheese and Wheat Thins. You, however, had the contacts."

"Hmm," Jack mused. He gazed out a rain-streaked window. "I suppose I did. Bill was the key, no doubt. It did take some convincing."

"That most certainly was one of Cindy's strongest talents." Immediately I wished I had not said that. Ever so slightly, I saw Jack wince and his eyes narrow. One can't go home again. We weren't the intimate college friends of old. Cindy, Bill's daughter, had been Jack's first wife, but the knot had come unraveled in the brutal realization that she, his high-school sweetheart, had a lover. With it dissolved all the security, structure, and exclusivity of an elite, small-town upbringing.

"I'll be damned," Jack said, glancing toward the entrance. "It's Rex Larry!"

I turned to see Rex, the pub's owner, removing his camelhair overcoat and a silk scarf, hanging them nonchalantly on the coat rack near the door. He moved to the bar where the bartender, who'd seen him enter, handed him a steaming coffee mug. Larry made a comment and the bartender laughed, too readily. Our waitress placed her tray on the bar, hugged Rex, and kissed his cheek. He took it as a matter of course, a perk of the successful publican.

"Does your secretary greet you like that?" I asked.

"Hardly," said Jack. "Office decorum would shatter in such a display of affection. I noticed that Rex was not in any anguish."

The waitress loaded her tray with our drinks and with the same confident, casual style set them before us. I was faster at finding my wallet than Jack—perhaps the difference between a salesman accustomed to treating customers and an attorney who gives away nothing.

Jack took a deep pull from his bourbon and seven; I did the same from my beer. We each sat back, saying nothing. I thought to myself that young girls no longer brought promise; they had become a forbidden temptation. Career choices had narrowed life's possibilities. The limitless horizon of youth had shrunk to a narrow path of responsibility. The adventure we had shared now blurred in the fog of routine.

"Do you recall exactly how you pulled it off?" I commented, more to break the silence than from an inability to recall the facts.

"First, we were lucky," said Jack, his eyes brightening, "and we were ready."

CHAPTER II

INCEPTION

Some years ago—never mind how long precisely—having little or no money in my purse, and nothing particular to interest me on shore, I thought I would sail about a little and see the watery part of the world.
—Herman Melville, *Moby Dick*

In our last year of college, the Vietnam war and the military draft cast a black pall on the future. With the Mi Lai slaughters stacked against the crumbling rationalizations of the military solution, our spring 1970 graduation meant the end of the college deferment and draconian decisions: be drafted, go to jail, flee to Canada, enlist in the National Guard, or file as a conscientious objector. Just getting a job or going to graduate school became high risk choices in those tortured days.

As was my usual, I walked out of the school's library at 11:30 p.m. The penetrating, cold mist condensed droplets from tree branches. My '66 Volkswagen Beetle was easy to spot in the empty parking lot. I let the engine idle a long while in the hope that the weak defroster might clear a tiny half-moon of visibility through the fog on the windshield. The glass and the future remained obscure this night.

Even though the windshield wipers whacked away at the rain, on-coming car lights blurred off wet pavement as I wound along Palatine Hill Road toward the ramshackle student rental we called the Pit House. I had rejected the clamor and banality of dorm life long ago in favor of off-campus housing.

The Pit House perched on the side of a ravine, not unusual in this hilly area of Portland. The house remained an architectural curiosity, however, because the construction put the roof level with the adjacent street. When standing at the narrow street-side parking, one's eye leveled at the drain gutter. Further, with time, the house had begun to tilt, giving the impression that at any moment it might toboggan down into the nearby ravine. Switching off the engine, I grabbed my book bag, quit the cold car, and leaped down the three large steps to the front door. Jack's desk occupied one side of the low-ceilinged living room.

"Progress?" he asked, relieved at the chance to break from his studies.

"Some," I grunted, shaking droplets from my coat and swinging the book bag onto the tattered couch. We made for the kitchen, which overlooked the ravine at a level downhill from the living room. From the old Frigidaire, I grabbed the well-hewn stub of a two-pound block of Tillamook cheddar cheese. Jack rummaged in the cupboard for the box of Wheat Thins.

"Anything new?" I asked after the first bite of cheddar was down.

"Not much," Jack said, munching and watching the rain streak the kitchen windows. "Oh yeah, Westgate is building two king crabbers at Bender Marine in Mobile."

"No kidding. Westgate is going into king crabbing?" I asked.

Jack and his girlfriend Cindy came from Astoria, Oregon. Her father Bill had been an executive with Bumble Bee when huge tuna drove north along the West Coast in great numbers. Astoria had been Bumble Bee's hub. But after years of overfishing, the schools of tuna dwindled. When Bumble Bee closed its Astoria operation, Bill went to work as an executive for Westgate. The company had various fishing interests, including tuna in Puerto Rico.

"That's a growing industry," Jack mumbled.

"Sure is. The skipper of the seiner I was on last summer in Kodiak works winters on a king crabber. Crabbing starts in December when weather is hell in the Bering Sea, but the pay is terrific."

Jack and I had the sea in common. Astoria, the oldest American settlement west of the Mississippi, possessed a long maritime history. I grew up on one of the San Juan Islands of Washington State. My college funds were earned during summers in Alaska commercial salmon fishing while Jack worked in the old Bumble Bee icehouse supplying the remaining coastal fishing fleet.

"Why are they having the boats built in the Gulf?" I asked.

"Well," said Jack, munching more cheese, "I heard that Northwest yards have full order books and Bender wants into the king crab boat market."

"Wonder if they can build boats down there tough enough for the Aleutian winter?"

"I guess the boats are all steel, for starters," Jack said absently.

"How will they get the boats to Alaska?" I asked.

"Oh, they have to be delivered through the Panama Canal and up the West Coast to Seattle for final outfitting. Cindy said that one will be ready to sail before Christmas. Bill will be down there next week, checking on their progress."

"Wouldn't it be great to be on the delivery crew?" I envisioned the turquoise Caribbean bathed in warm sunshine.

Jack stopped chewing and turned toward me. I stopped chewing as the idea germinated.

"Do you think we could get on as crew?" I asked.

"Maybe," said Jack slowly. "Just maybe . . ."

CHAPTER III
FLIGHT TO MOBILE

Two weeks had passed since the rainy night when we ate cheese and dreamed of the warm Caribbean Sea. Occasionally, late at night, we speculated about the voyage, what it might be like standing wheel watch while crossing a sun-drenched sea. Beyond these fleeting discussions, we seldom mentioned the trip. Superstitious, we feared too much talk could anger spiteful Fate, who would obliterate our chances for the voyage.

Term papers and finals dominated every moment of fall quarter's last weeks. With the last exam completed on a Friday afternoon in December, I drove back to the Pit House feeling drained and hungry for a pizza.

"We got it," Jack yelled as I opened the front door. "The crew—it's us! They got a captain and engineer for one of the boats, but with delivery during Christmas they couldn't get anyone else for crew. So we're going!"

Jack threw himself on the couch, shielding his eyes from imagined sunlight. "Oh, I can feel that warm Caribbean sun on my face!"

"You're not kidding me, are you?" I asked.

"Kidding you? Kidding you? I would not joke about this. We'll even be paid in addition to room and board, maybe $600 for the entire voyage. That is $600 each. Kidding—hell, no. We're going to sea!"

"Son of a bitch! Ah, the Caribbean—the palm trees—and the Panama Canal—that will be fantastic. Just imagine transiting the Panama!" I jumped up and down, trying not to hit my head on the low ceiling of the living room.

Jack vaulted from the couch, dived into his bedroom, and rummaged in his closet. He emerged with sunglasses on and flung himself back onto the couch.

"Don't bother me," he said, turning his face to the imaginary sun, "I'm on the back deck in the lounge chair sunning myself. I'm off watch. You're on watch."

"Jack, I'm going to love being on watch. I've heard these king crabbers are really sophisticated boats. She'll have all the latest navigational gear including LORAN. I'd love to learn to use LORAN."

"LORAN? How does that work?" he asked, rousing from his imaginary chaise lounge.

"Radio waves broadcast from shore, I think. The LORAN compares two sets of incoming signals and can tell you exactly where you are within maybe a hundred feet or so. Well, that's a guess. I hope the captain is an amiable sort and will take some time to show us how to navigate."

"Hmmm," mumbled Jack, "The captain and the engineer—unknown quantities. Their personalities will affect how things go."

"Yeah, a captain's word is law on the sea, even today," I said. "The voyage isn't that long. Besides, it's a delivery, so all we do is get the boat to the West Coast. We don't have to go king crabbing."

"They both have to be licensed, so they must know their stuff. I'm sure Westgate isn't going to hire a couple of incompetents," said Jack defending the wisdom of his girlfriend's executive father.

"Jesus, when do we leave?" I asked, grabbing Jack's sunglasses. I stuck them on my nose but still shaded my eyes from the imaginary glare.

"Well, the boat should be finished before Christmas. We may sail just before Christmas or maybe the day after. The schedule isn't totally set."

"How long does this trip take anyway? I hope it's done before the winter term starts," I said, concerned about tight timing.

"I asked," said Jack. "It'll take about three to four days from Mobile to Panama, then a day through the Canal and about a week to San Diego."

"That sounds doable," I said, "but we have some leeway as winter term doesn't begin until January 7th."

"Plus, we can get the first week of assignments for each class, buy the books before we go, and do the reading so we're not behind at all even if we miss a day or two."

"Great idea! We'll have to be in touch over Christmas break so we can coordinate the departure."

"No problem. Bill will be home before Christmas. He'll have the plane tickets. I'll pick them up from him in Astoria. We'll leave together from Portland."

"Jack, for a guy who seemed cool to this trip, you sure have been working on the details," I observed.

"What do you mean 'cool'!" said Jack, grabbing the dark glasses back. "I saw it as a golden opportunity. It just needed the master's touch to put it all together."

"Oh right. I thought I recognized Cindy's hand in all this."

Jack threw the lone couch pillow at my head.

☸

The expectation of steaming over the sunny Caribbean Sea took on a special aura. Fate offered Jack and me this sea voyage, like the eye of the storm, a momentary escape from the cyclone of the Vietnam war.

Jack called on the first day of Christmas break. The vessel completion schedule had slipped a few days, but the significance went unnoticed in the glare of our optimism. Then it slipped again, to the day after Christmas. We calculated we could still complete the delivery to San Diego before classes began in January.

"OK, OK," I said to Jack over the phone. "I'll call you on the 22nd. By then the plane tickets should be set and you let me know when to be at Portland International."

"Right," said Jack, "And if anything changes, I'll call again."

The vacation days passed in intense expectation. I frequented the fisheries supply stores in Seattle and my hometown to augment the gear I used in the summer salmon fishery. These stores served commercial fishermen, not weekend anglers. The aisles smelled of oilcloth. The shelves were stocked with heavy woolens, orange rubber gloves, and tough Norwegian rain gear. Customers in Seattle chandleries didn't worry about hot weather. The challenge lay in finding garments light enough for southern seas.

I made several small purchases, then one grand one: a pair of Irish Setter leather boots by Red Wing, expensive but high quality. They had the oil-resistant soles preferred by commercial fishermen and could be easily pulled on after a day's fishing when the heavy rubber boots came off. The Setter's sole, having no heel, gripped slippery surfaces and would not catch on lines or netting. I advised Jack what to take and told him I had purchased the Red Wings.

Christmas finally arrived. We flew out the night of December 25, and the Portland Airport was deserted. Jack and I were ecstatic, but our girlfriends, seeing us off at the airport, were not so excited.

"After all, the voyage is only a delivery," I told my girlfriend Alice, who had become my confidant. "Summer fishing in Kodiak is far more danger-ous. Nothing major will go wrong."

"Still, it seems dumb," said Alice, "Be careful. Don't be one of those guys who falls overboard at night, never to be seen again."

"This will be a tropical cruise, a piece of cake," I said.

Jack was having a similar discussion with Cindy, even though she had helped set up the voyage.

"Hey, this is a new boat. What can go wrong? The captain and engineer are licensed. Your dad wouldn't hire a couple of slouches. Are you sure you're not just a little jealous?"

"No, I'm not," said Cindy. "Going to sea in a fishing boat is not my idea of a cruise! And you better not fool around in those port towns along the way, either!"

"Not my style," said Jack, as the boarding announcement for our flight was called.

Jack and I hurriedly kissed our girlfriends goodbye and headed down the jetway. On the Continental Stretch 727, we found our assigned seats toward the back in the main cabin. We settled in, elated, even though getting to Mobile was going to be tortuous. The first part of the routing, Portland–Seattle–Houston, would get us into Houston at 1:00 a.m. In Houston, however, we had a long layover, not leaving until 5:30 a.m., and then we had to change planes in New Orleans before getting to Mobile. The company selected the route to save money. That first night, however, Jack and I were oblivious to the routing; the adventure had begun. The plane taxied into the black night, found its way to the active runway, and rocketed into the low overcast for the short hop to Seattle.

In Seattle, only two passengers boarded. To add to our good fortune, an attractive female flight attendant came back and announced to the handful of economy-class passengers that we would be the guests of Continental Airlines in the first-class cabin. The long plane, so lightly loaded, needed weight forward. Jack winked and I could not suppress a broad smile as we settled into the wide, leather, first-class seats. The jet climbed into the night sky. Soon the flight attendant was back.

"What would you like to drink?" she asked. Jack was ready.

"Bourbon and seven," he said, in a routine, matter-of-fact manner.

"And you?" she said to me with a dazzlingly white smile.

"The same," I answered, but slowly, judiciously, to emphasize that I was contemplating the correct choice for the occasion.

"We're in first class," Jack chortled as soon as the attendant stepped into the galley. "These are on the house!" And so they were, all of them, all the way to Houston.

Who can say exactly what it was: the proximity to Christmas or the late-night, nearly empty flight. The holiday mood had infected the flight attendants. They congregated in the first-class section, talking and laughing and making sure that each passenger had enough Christmas cheer. The flight had become a party.

Jack, tall and trim with fair hair, sat in an aisle seat. The young flight attendant with the flashing smile lingered longer and longer in her conversations with him. Eventually she sat on the arm of the aisle seat opposite him, her long legs crossed. Jack had to twist in his seat to talk to her, his neck constantly turned to the right. At one point he reached back and unconsciously began rubbing his neck. She stood and began to massage his shoulder muscles. His visible relaxation at her touch only encouraged deeper kneading. I ordered another bourbon and seven.

The party ended at 1:00 a.m. as we entered the new Houston International Terminal with its punishingly bright lights. We had vaguely considered finding a room for the hours between this arrival and our departure. Now we were serious. Standing before a back-lit screen with glaring advertisements, we squinted, attempting to discern, through the welter of room pictures and promises of comfort, which hotel was closest to the airport. Our growing drowsiness warned that we minimize transit and maximize sleep time, and we did not dare miss our connecting flight.

Nothing was making sense. Our dilemma was verging on paralysis when our flight crew happened by.

"Thaay," Jack slurred, picking out his flight attendant friend. His pronunciation was that of a dental patient loaded with Novocain. "Thaay, we need a nearby hotel for the night 'cause we've got an early flight tomorrow."

"Actually, it's today," I said attempting to clarify everything, but only achieving an Abbott and Costello effect causing some of the crewmembers to chuckle. Jack's new friend mercifully took us under her wing.

"Follow us. The hotel we use is as close as any. I'm sure it's not full," she said, with that flashing smile. Everything struck me as too bright in Texas.

I stumbled into one of the hotel van's bench seats, sitting wedged into the corner by the captain. Conscious of my alcohol-laden breath, I faced the window, saying nothing. We drove for what seemed like miles and miles to the hotel. Jack sat next to the flight attendant and chatted the whole way.

By the time we reached the hotel's hacienda portico, I was panicked that we could not get back to the airport in time for our next flight. When disembarking, I asked the driver if the van ran all night. He said it did. Jack disembarked next and asked him exactly the same question. He looked closely at the two of us.

"Must be an echo," he said laconically.

"Huh?" Jack asked.

"We're not doing real well," I said, dragging Jack toward the front desk.

If Jack was bewildered by the comments of the van driver, he was broken-hearted by the sudden disappearance of the flight crew once we were inside the hotel. We had only begun to register when they were handed room keys and were gone. We ordered a wake-up call at 4:15 a.m. and staggered off to our room.

Although the bourbon made us drowsy at the airport, sleep proved elusive when we had settled into our room. I lay with my arms behind my head. Jack speculated about the amount of tan he would get on the voyage. Each time I shut my eyes, thoughts welled up about the war. What could I do with a draft number of 186? Carlin Capper-Johnson, one of our professors, had stood before the assemblage on the administration lawn describing being a conscientious objector in England in World War I and being imprisoned as a consequence. He had then witnessed the Second World War and the Korean War and now the Vietnam War. He was convinced that war could

13

be ended but only when the young men who always fight the old men's wars simply refused to fight.

"What will you do after school, Jack?" I asked.

"Wow! No more thoughts of the war," Jack commanded. "We're in Houston on our way to the Caribbean. Only a few short weeks ago, this was but a dream and we were booking it to get through finals. This is heaven."

"Agreed, this is the life. Of course, you got the back rub, but she smiled most persuasively at me." A pillow slammed into my face.

I tossed and turned, as did Jack, until the jangling wake-up call. The shower helped, but the inside of my eye lids felt like sandpaper by the time the van deposited us back at the still gleaming airport.

Jack and I were herded, like bovines, onto the flight to New Orleans. The plane was nearly full, the stewardess perfunctory. The coffee served had the rich aroma of day-old dishwater—no back rubs, either.

Killing time before the final leg, we walked out onto a deck above the New Orleans terminal. The humidity intensified the morning heat into a sultry haze that squeezed sweat from our polluted pores. The flight routing, inconsequential yesterday, achieved, in the dripping humidity, a persistent water torture effect.

The flight from New Orleans to Mobile compared the first-class luxury of the Stretch 727 to that of the stench and claustrophobia of a Greyhound bus. The plane, an old propeller DC-6, was crammed with rumpled businessmen, looking as though they had flown all night from Chicago. I sat near the back next to an obese, balding, red-faced man whose act of breathing threatened to squeeze me out of my aisle seat. The rising hot air outside generated thermals that slammed the laboring plane up and down, adding nausea to the misery of sweat dribbling down my forehead.

The DC-6 slammed onto the Mobile tarmac and rolled to a stop before a tiny, bedraggled box of a terminal. Only Jack and I deplaned. The plane's door slammed shut behind us. The engines coughed back to life and the plane rattled into the air as we collected our bags at the outdoor luggage rack. We stood curbside waiting for the limousine to the Admiral Semmes Motel. A damp wind blew.

CHAPTER IV

THE CAPTAIN AND THE ENGINEER

> "And once for all, let me tell thee and assure thee, young man, it's better
> to sail with a moody good captain than a laughing bad one."
>
> —Herman Melville, *Moby Dick*

The trees in the nearby forest rose to a uniform height and collectively scribed a flat line across the monotonous horizon. The wind, cooler than in New Orleans, sucked the heat from our sleep-deprived bodies. We began to shiver. Jack went back into the terminal to call the limousine service a second time.

While Jack was still in the terminal, a car rumbled into view, a vision from another era. The early 1950s black Cadillac limousine, with a visor extending low over the front window, careened on worn shocks around a long curve. Its V8 engine grumbled loudly through a disintegrating exhaust system. No one was visible behind the wheel. I stood my ground, despite the sensation that this vehicle was the automotive equivalent of the headless horseman. When the car arrived curbside, I saw, with relief, a diminutive Black man was piloting this monstrosity, peering through the space between the steering wheel and the dashboard.

"Y'all goin' to the Admiral Semmes, suh?" he asked as he popped out from the driver's side door.

"Yes," I said, still amazed that such a tiny personage could coax this behemoth down the road.

"Wasn't they two of you?"

"Oh sure, my friend is in calling again. I'll go get him."

My reference to a second call cast a frown across the driver's face, but he said nothing. As I turned, Jack came out of the terminal. The little man, with ant-like strength, grabbed our heavy bags and aligned them neatly in the cavernous trunk.

Jack and I sat in the once-luxurious leather back seat, which was now worn and musty. We wound our way from the airport into the heart of Mobile. The gray day and humid wind emphasized the decay of once-white pillared houses that haunted tree-lined streets. Paint peeled from them while rot ate at the bases of their formerly sturdy columns. Torn front door screens flapped in the persistent wind.

As if inherited from our environs, a depression settled upon us. Neither Jack nor I spoke. Finally, the limo swayed into the downtown area, leaned around a corner, and stopped in the portico of a flat-roofed, four-story structure painted gray green. The sign out front read the Admiral Semmes Motor Inn. Apparently, the Admiral had been one of Mobile's most illustrious contributions to the Confederacy. This namesake motel was anything but illustrious, however. The driver quickly unloaded the bags onto a porter's cart, accepted our tip, and drove off, leaving clouds of blue smoke in his wake.

The reception area was cold, both in temperature and in its stark emptiness. A large Black porter wrestled the luggage cart through the door. We waited at the reception counter. No one was present so Jack rang the desk bell. Nothing happened. We waited. Jack reached up to ring the bell again, but the porter warned softly, "She comin' when she ready."

The subtle pronouncement froze Jack's hand, and he pulled it back slowly. We waited. A door opened and a heavy-set white woman appeared. Moving in a deliberate shuffle to the counter, she opened a drawer, took out two registration cards, and placed them in front of us. She finally looked at us, her eyes beady and narrowed.

"Y'all are with Westgate, isn't that so?" She knew the answer.

"Yes," I said, as cheerfully as possible. A slight sneer of disdain curled her upper lip.

"We're expecting a couple of other fellows from Westgate. Have they arrived yet?" asked Jack, ignoring the frosty atmosphere.

She didn't answer, but reached behind into a cubbyhole, then turned and slapped a folded piece of paper on the counter. Jack read the note.

"The captain and engineer are not staying here but have checked into the Ramada. The captain left a phone number to call," said Jack.

"You two have a car?" she asked.

"No, we will be staying here," said Jack.

"Fill these out and be sure to sign them," she ordered.

She gathered our registration cards, double-checking that we had signed them. Then she dropped two keys onto the countertop.

"Willis," she said to the porter, "show them to their room." She walked back through the door from which she had entered, slamming it shut behind her.

Willis motioned us to the lone elevator. The three of us squeezed in alongside the luggage cart. Willis hit the fourth-floor button. The elevator doors closed slowly, with the sound of metal grating on metal.

Arriving at the second floor, we walked down a long hall with a worn carpet to our room. Willis waited patiently for his tip, then left, the sound of a squeaky wheel on his cart fading down the hall. I locked the door.

"Wow," I said, noting the stains on the room's popcorn ceiling. "If this is southern hospitality, I am glad they weren't mad at us."

"Charming, wasn't she?" said Jack. "The captain and engineer stopped here but decided to find a more upscale motel. She feels cheated out of half her business and let us know about it."

"Yeah, the place seems empty, so maybe she lost fifty percent of her business for the week," I mused.

Jack had moved to the telephone, but hovered his hand over it, not lifting the receiver.

"Do you think I should call him now?" Jack asked, furtively.

"We have to contact him. The sooner the better."

"I know but—," Jack answered, "I don't want to disturb him."

"It's one in the afternoon—how are you going to disturb him?" I said, growing frustrated by Jack's timidity.

"Well, maybe he and the engineer had to fly all night like we did. They could be sleeping."

"Look, even so, he can't get too angry about a call at this time of day. Besides, he may want to know if we made it here OK." My frustration over this debate entered my voice.

"You call him," said Jack moving away from the phone.

"OK," I answered, walking toward the phone, but I began to think about the importance of this first contact. What would the captain be like? His nature would dramatically influence the character of the voyage. This was a person whose body language mattered, which would be impossible to observe over the phone.

"Not so easy?" asked Jack, observing my ambivalence.

"I see what you mean. I wish we could meet this guy face to face before we call him." I paused for yet another second, then lifted the receiver. "He is going to be the way he is, and we have to find that out sooner than later."

I dialed and asked for Dean Alexander. The phone in his room rang and rang. No answer.

"Not there," I announced with some relief. "Checked in but not in his room."

Jack moved to look out the window. I followed. Gray clouds overhung the drab town. The wind blew a strong draft in around the window's metal frame.

While I hunted for the room's heat control, the fatigue of travel and the dull remnants of hangover overtook me. The escape from school was behind us. The voyage with the unknown personalities of the captain and engineer loomed ahead. The room was deadly quiet before the heating fan rattled to life, creating a loud racket that hardly moved the room's musty air. We unpacked, then dropped onto our beds.

Night had fallen by the time we woke. The rattling and clanking fan had not warmed the room. While Jack showered, I peered out the rain-streaked window. Although we had flown south more than halfway across the country, the weather appeared to be as cold and wet as in Portland. Feeling desolate, I sat on the edge of the sway-backed bed.

Jack, wrapped in a white towel, emerged from the bathroom in a cloud of steam. He smiled for the first time since the flight attendant had massaged his back.

"Oh man, the shower," he said. "The water is hot. I feel like a new man."

I fought my way into the steamy bathroom, wondering if the intensity of Jack's shower had caused the paint to peel from the bathroom ceiling or if it had been that way for some time. The hot water emphasized how chilled I had become. I let it cascade over my shoulders a good while before I soaped down. After the shower, I wiped the mist from the mirror and shaved. These rituals dissolved the crust of travel fatigue. I dressed quickly to stay warm in the cold bedroom.

"You hungry?" I asked Jack, who was reading *Newsweek* on his bed.

"Yes, but what about the captain and engineer?" he asked.

"I called last time. Your turn."

He rotated to a sitting position and reached for the phone, then stopped. "Look, we'll be with these guys for the next three weeks. Let's grab a bite and call them when we get back." I agreed.

We wanted to escape the motel to eat. Dinner was in a worn-down cafe we found around a corner. Judging from the stares we received, we might have been the first foreigners in the place since the carpetbaggers who arrived on the heels of the Union Army. The unremarkable food was suspended in a formidable grease. So far, southern hospitality and southern cooking shared indigestibility.

Back in our room, Jack went directly to the phone, dialed the Ramada, and got through to the captain's room. Jack spoke in his official, mature tone, pitched an octave lower than his natural voice.

"Hi, I'm Jack. Steve and I got in this morning. How was your trip? Yes, ours was, too. Rundown? Absolutely. Is the Ramada far? Rental car? Yes, we want to see the boat. See you at 8:30 a.m. here. Sounds good. Right, we'll be ready to work. Goodbye."

"Well, how does he sound?" I asked when Jack hung up the phone.

"He sounds like a good guy. They didn't like the look of the Semmes when they got here. They have a rental car for provisioning the boat, so they drove to a couple of other hotels and picked the Ramada because it's new. Sounds like it's a few miles out of town, but we don't have that option."

"Do you think he'll teach us navigation?" I asked.

"Sounds like he wouldn't have any objection. He's easy to talk to."

"Sounds like we're heading for the shipyard in the morning. Great," I said, in a resurgence of optimism.

"Yeah, they'll pick us up here. He told us to bring our coveralls and be ready for work."

"Coveralls, have you even got any?" I asked.

"I had them laid out, but they wouldn't fit in my luggage," Jack replied, but he couldn't keep a straight face.

Elated by tomorrow's prospects, we even did some class reading before we turned in.

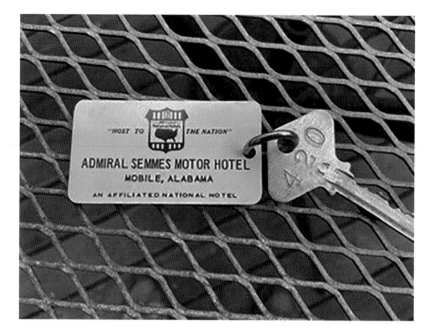

Our room key at the Admiral Semmes Motor Inn. Photo by Jack.

☸

The combination of a good night's sleep and the exciting prospects of the coming day awakened us early. We arrived at the motel dining room in high spirits and famished. The dining room was not in high spirits, however. The drab character of the motel extended into this stark room with metal-legged tables and chairs. The vinyl upholstery of the chairs, hardened and cracked, oozed over the seats like brittle frosting over stale cupcakes. A few men hunched over cups of coffee.

We dutifully waited at the "Please Wait to Be Seated" sign until a wisp of a waitress passed by and said, "Sit anywhere, but if y'all are in a hurry, sit at the counter."

We sat at a table. The waitress returned, splashed weak coffee into our cups, and took our orders, writing nothing down. We both ordered the All-American Breakfast: bacon, eggs, and pancakes.

"Did you order mashed potatoes?" I asked Jack after the waitress set down the plates in front of us. Beside the bacon and eggs was a mound of white mush with a pat of butter melting into it.

Jack, taking a dab on the end of a spoon, tried the mush.

"Grits," he said. "The South—grits."

"They're not mentioned on the menu. I guess you just get them," I said.

The grits tasted starchy, like humid air from a freshly plastered room. Butter was mandatory for taste. The weighty pancakes, stacked on a side plate, also packed flesh on our bones.

By 8:20 a.m. we were waiting in the lobby, ready to go. Dressed in our work clothes, we were prepared for a day's work, readying the boat for the long-awaited voyage. We were still ready and waiting at 8:30 and at 8:45 and at 9:00 and at 9:30.

"Perhaps he meant they would meet us at the boat yard?" I asked Jack.

"No, the captain said he would meet us here at the Admiral Semmes," Jack said emphatically.

"Of course, we could call him," I said, "but that won't be good if he's still in his room. Maybe he is tied up on the phone with Westgate?"

"No," Jack said. "He can't be on the phone this long."

We waited silently for another fifteen minutes. We had occupied the lobby for over an hour. Willis had acknowledged our presence long ago. This delay, we felt, made even Willis a little disdainful of us. Nobody important waits so long in the lobby of the Admiral Semmes. Jack relented and went to the pay phone, located just off the lobby. He returned after a few minutes to report that no one answered in the captain's room.

We were not accustomed to waiting. Most events in the college world went strictly by the clock and the calendar. Wavelets of doubt lapped at our sandcastle of optimism.

Suddenly a red Mercury Cougar motored into the motel's portico. A short, stocky fellow with dark hair and a goatee got out of the passenger side and entered, heading for the front desk. Rolled tightly under his arm were coveralls. This had to be one of our team, so we intercepted him.

"Are you the engineer for the *Scottie*?" I asked, offering my hand. "I'm Steve and this is Jack. We're the crew."

"OK," said the engineer, extending his hand to shake mine. His grip was weak and the skin of his hand felt soft. "I'm Henry. Well, are you ready to go?"

"Sure," we said in unison, sounding like two parrots. Henry ambled out to the waiting Cougar and held the door while Jack and I climbed into the cramped back seat. I wondered for an instant how this two-door car would haul the supplies needed to provision the boat for a 25-day voyage.

"Hi," said the driver, extending his hand awkwardly toward the back seat. "Dean Alexander. I'm the skipper for this little jaunt to the West Coast." His handshake was perfunctory and limp, maybe because he had to cramp around in the bucket seat. Henry settled himself comfortably into the front passenger seat. As soon as the door shut, Dean gunned the engine and we roared away from the Admiral Semmes.

"Well," said Dean, the boom still in his voice, "How do you two like Mobile?"

"We haven't seen much of it yet," Jack offered, "but it doesn't seem bursting with activity."

"'Not bursting with activity'—hear that, Henry—you got that right," said Dean, lighting up a cigarette with the car's lighter as we shot along the quiet Mobile streets. "Yeah, not much here all in all, but Henry and I found a pretty good spot last night and we heard about another with a live Dixieland band. Do you guys like music?"

"Sure," I said, but before I could offer an opinion on Dixieland, Dean disclosed, in a conspiratorial hush, a facet of his partnership with Henry.

"Henry and I've been together for a while. The trumpeter here's got his own band in Seattle. We've been in some great places with that horn, right, Henry?"

"For sure," said Henry, "As a matter of fact, I was working on a great New Year's gig when Dean called about this trip. The band wasn't happy when I told them I was heading for the Caribbean, but what the hell, Dean talked me into it."

Before Henry could say more, the rocketing Cougar bounced violently over a set of railroad tracks, with everyone flailing for a handhold. Then the sign came into view: BENDER SHIPYARD. Dean swung the careening Cougar up to the entry gate, stopping at a small guard shack. A pot-bellied watchman, having scurried into the gate shack at our thundering approach, leaned out a tiny window. Dean exclaimed loudly that he was captain of the new king crabber *Scottie* and that we were here to see the boat. This had the desired effect: the watchman waved us on immediately. Dean gave a quick side wink to Henry, taking inflated credit for the watchman's recognition of a captain's status.

The boatyard centered itself around three large open sheds. Historically, the principal business of this yard had been the construction of commercial

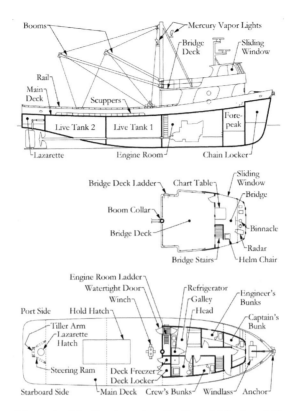

Schematic of the *Scottie,* produced by Brent J. Morrison, NA

shrimp boats. Kaiser had pioneered an assembly line production technique for Liberty ships in World War II, and Bender had copied it. The steel shrimper hulls were made in three sections—bow, middle and stern—each under its own shed. These sections were then welded together. A hodgepodge of equipment, from forklifts to rusting pick-up trucks filled with welding gear, populated spaces between the sheds. No one appeared to be working.

Scottie was tied at one of Bender's finger piers. At nearly 90 feet long, with the deck house forward, she had a large open main deck for transporting and working the king crab pots. A hatch cover topped each of the two live tanks. These tanks, when pumped full of circulating seawater, kept the crab alive until processed. The bridge, sitting forward on top of the deck house, stretched from one side of the vessel to the other, offering good visibility. The anchor windlass occupied the small triangle of deck forward of the deck house.

M/V STEVIE—A 91' x 24' x 12' steel king crab vessel built for Point Adams Packing Company by Bender Shipbuilding of Mobile, Alabama recently joined the North Pacific king crab fleet. The vessel will be skippered by Lee Cowan of Kodiak, Alaska. She is powered by one Caterpillar 379 Marine Diesel, and has two auxiliary Caterpillar D330 75 KW generator sets.

The *Stevie*, sister ship of the *Scottie*. *Fisherman's News*, February 1970, second issue

The all-stainless galley and the head with shower and stacked washer and dryer occupied the aft section of the deck house. A passageway lead from the galley forward to the base of the stairs to the bridge, with one crew cabin on each side of the passage. Each cabin had a bunk bed with storage for two crew, providing unheard-of luxury. In the boats I had fished on, the crew was stacked into bunks in a crowded forecastle below decks. Forward of the deck level crew cabins, the entire area under the bridge was the captain's stateroom.

In the Alaskan purse seine fishery, the size of the boat was limited to 58 feet, giving the generic term "limit seiner." Many of these vessels were built of wood. By comparison, our first impression of the steel-hulled *Scottie* was of a huge, powerful, and even luxurious vessel.

We explored on board for over an hour, but no workers arrived to show us around. The entire yard remained eerily empty.

CHAPTER V
THE LONG DELAY

It seemed as though we had been forgotten by the world, belonged to nobody, would get nowhere; . . .

—Joseph Conrad, *Youth*

My eyes adjusted to the light coming through a slit in the drawn curtains. Lying on my back, I studied the ceiling. I turned on my side, looking though the crack in the curtains. The sky was still gray. The troubling question bubbled again to consciousness: would we ever make this voyage?

When we had parted the night before, neither the captain nor the engineer had set a work plan for today. Jack and I, wishing to avoid impertinence toward our marine superiors, had avoided raising questions of work.

"I thought you'd never come to," said Jack.

I rolled over. Jack was staring at the ceiling. How long had he been awake?

He rolled over, looking out the crack in the curtains.

"The weather hasn't changed?" I asked.

"I think we made a mistake last night not forcing the question of work for today," said Jack, propping his head up on an elbow.

"Yeah, but the captain was not in the mood to discuss business," I said.

"The captain went after the first skirt in the place, even though she was well past her prime. He sure blew it when he said he liked soul music. Her type is not into soul music," Jack laughed.

"Yep," I answered. "Obviously, Henry and Dean have been a team for a long time. I wonder if Dean has another position as a skipper and just takes deliveries to maintain his lifestyle?"

"I'm not sure," answered Jack. "I guess there's lots we don't know about the captain. What time is it?"

"Hmm . . . 8:15."

"Shower and breakfast," said Jack, getting up, "but breakfast may be a problem. Do we go out and risk missing a phone call from the skipper?"

"Given the amount he was drinking, I don't think the skipper will call this early."

"No, but let's not part company with him again without setting a schedule for the next day," Jack concluded.

Breakfast came and went. We read in the room until almost 1:00 p.m., and faced the same dilemma about lunch as we had about breakfast: should we go out to eat or not?

"Look, I think we better give him a call. Maybe he expects initiative. We don't want to get off on a bad foot," I said.

Jack thought for a minute. "Yeah, I think you're right, but you give him the call."

I did. The phone rang and rang. I almost hung up when Dean finally answered.

"Hello?" came his groggy voice.

"Hello, skipper. This is Steve. Will we need to be at the yard today?" Jack winced at my abrupt words, but I couldn't think of another way to broach the subject.

"We . . . aah . . . what time is it?" Dean asked.

"About 1:30 p.m."

"Right," he said, then after a long pause, spoke again: "No, the yard won't want us in the way. You boys take the rest of the day off, but we'll pick you up at 10:00 a.m. tomorrow at the Semmes. We'll begin provisioning."

"OK, fine," I said, "Goodbye."

"Well?" asked Jack.

"We have the rest of the day off, but they will pick us up here tomorrow at 10:00 to start provisioning."

"OK," said Jack. "I guess there is nothing much going on at the yard."

"He was still sleeping, which means he couldn't have called the yard yet today," I said.

"Hmm, I guess we have another free day in Mobile," said Jack.

After lunch we walked in the now familiar run-down environs around the Admiral Semmes—familiar enough to know they offered nothing for us. Back in the room, we read. Logic class, a requirement for my major, was ahead for me. I thought I understood the first chapter. Dusk came, reminding us that another day had ended with no departure date set.

For dinner, we walked a long distance, but ended up in a cafe of the same quality as the ones close to the Admiral Semmes. On the walk home, Jack and I speculated that perhaps Mobile's suburbs were livelier than her moribund heart. Without a car—and we did not dare rent one—we stood little chance of finding out.

Despite the growing threat of delay, we arose the next morning in much better spirits. At least by 10:00 a.m., we would start provisioning. We were up and mushing through grits well before 8:00.

"Wonder how we will provision the boat?" I asked.

"Well, I don't know," mumbled Jack, swallowing a mouthful. "I would guess an experienced captain like Dean has done this before. Maybe he and Henry have a check list."

We waited in the lobby until we could stand Willis's scrutiny no longer. At 11:00, we returned to our room.

"Get the pattern?" asked Jack.

"It certainly is a pattern," I said. "They haven't been on time yet, but I'm not going to call. He gave us the time and the place. We'll just hold here until they show up."

For lunch we ate at the Admiral Semmes' restaurant, not wanting to leave for fear we would miss them. At 1:00 p.m. we returned to our room and read.

"At this rate," I said, looking up from the logic text, "I will have read most of the books for next term before we depart."

"At this rate," responded Jack, "we will be back in class before the *Scottie* leaves Mobile. I'll call Cindy tonight to find out about the company's schedule for this boat."

Before Jack could say more, the phone rang.

"Hello," said Jack. "Yes, we're ready. We'll be right down." He hung up.

"They're in the lobby. He asked if we were ready for a little provisioning work!" said Jack. We grabbed our jackets and bolted from the room, elated to be doing something to hasten our departure.

"Hi, men," said Dean, as we piled again into the back of the Cougar, but he then continued his conversation with Henry.

"I tell you, she was a rocket, but she just wouldn't come back to my room. It needs a little more time. We're going back there tonight."

"OK," mumbled Henry.

Dean took a long drag on his cigarette and drummed his fingers impatiently on the steering wheel while waiting at a stoplight. As soon as it changed, the Cougar made another jack rabbit start.

"Well, boys," Dean said, coming back from his thoughts, "we're heading to Sears to get a few things for the boat."

CHAPTER VI
PROVISIONING

Every one knows what a multitude of things—beds, sauce-pans, knives and forks, shovels and tongs, napkins, nut-crackers, and what not, are indispensable to the business of housekeeping.

—Herman Melville, *Moby Dick*

The Cougar wheeled into the Sears Roebuck parking lot. As we entered the brown brick multistory building, Jack and I noticed that neither man carried notebooks. Led by Dean, we charged into the store.

"Where is the housewares department?" Dean demanded of the first woman he saw. The woman, who was clearly not a clerk, appeared visibly startled by the bellowed question.

"Are you speaking to me?" she asked, which exasperated the impatient captain, who was still assuming he was dealing with a store employee. "I believe it is on the second floor," she added indignantly.

"Right," said the captain. He veered off toward a bank of elevators, hammering the UP call button two or three times until he noticed a nearby stairwell.

"Come on," he said, leading the charge up one flight. By the time we arrived in the housewares department, Dean was out of breath; a fine bead of sweat glistened on his forehead.

"God damn, it's hot in here," he said. "OK, let's get started."

We stood in an aisle, pots and pans on one side and utensils of all sorts on the other.

"Here's something you always need in the galley but never can find on a boat," said Dean, grabbing a large whisk.

"Uh, huh," said Henry, "but maybe we should start with pots and pans. Let's see, we'll need one, three, and four-quart pans, but we're going to need a couple of big pots. Remember this is a king crabber."

Henry began selecting cookware while the captain collected an armful of whisks, spatulas, cooking spoons, and a potato peeler that he was proud to have remembered. Jack and I stood amazed. No items were being checked off an organized list. We were witnessing a raid on the kitchen department. Furthermore, if an item needed for the galley was not stocked on Sears' kitchenware shelves, it would not be on this boat. "Let's see," said Dean when a big whisk clattered to the floor from the load of utensils in his arms, "you guys find us some shopping carts."

Jack and I looked at each other, then dutifully set out to find carts. We found one with sheets piled in it and a pricing device. Jack said nothing but lifted the goods out and handed them to me.

"Oh, thanks," I said as I placed them on a nearby shelf.

"Boy," said Jack, "this is a novel approach. We've got the whole boat to outfit. You'd think these guys would contact the sales manager here to get the purchase organized, or arrange a volume discount, or something."

Unable to hold more, Dean impatiently awaited the cart. He dumped the utensils in with a crash. We followed him down the aisle to where Henry had an array of pots and pans laid out neatly on the floor. Dean ordered us to throw the pots and pans in. We struggled to hold the utensils to one side in the cart to keep them from being crushed by the weight of multiple cast-iron skillets. Dean kept throwing in more items. Henry made more judicious choices, all the while mumbling about properly equipping the galley of a commercial fishing boat.

The heap in the cart neared overflowing. Whether it was the disappearance of her cart or the shear mass of goods we were collecting, our actions attracted the attention of a woman with a Sears name tag on her blouse that read "Betty."

"Oh my," she said in a southern drawl, looking with widening eyes at the overburdened cart. "Y'all sure is buyin' a bunch."

"Yeah," answered Dean, pausing to light another cigarette, sweat running down his face in rivulets. "We're outfitting *Scottie* for her trip to Alaska," he announced in official tones.

"Alaska?" Betty asked. Then after a long pause, she carefully added, "And what's a *Scottie*?"

"That's the king crabber we're picking up at Bender. I'm the captain and these men are the crew." Dean took another long drag.

"Oh my," she said. "What y'all mean by a king crabber?"

"That's a boat for fishing big crab in the Bering Sea. It's coming from the Bender Yard here in Mobile. You know where Bender is, don't you?"

"Well, sir, I's not exactly sure," she said, looking confused but trying to follow this incongruent story coming from the sweaty white man who had more kitchen items in his cart then she usually sold in six months.

The skipper began to realize that this woman actually had no idea what he was talking about.

"Say, we're going to need another cart for the sheets and blankets. Can you get us another cart?"

"Oh, yes sir," she said. Relieved, she ambled off, mumbling to herself.

"Henry, are you about finished in this department?" Dean asked impatiently. "Jesus, its hot in here. Aren't you hot?"

This last question was directed at Jack and me. We nodded in agreement. A long moment of silence was broken when Betty returned with a white man in a polyester suit, with a tag on the left lapel that read "Roy, Sales Manager."

"Hello," drawled Roy, "my sales clerk here says y'all is buying a lot of items for a boat."

"Yep," said Dean, "we're outfitting the king crabber *Scottie* built by Bender here in Mobile. We're taking her around to Seattle."

Roy mulled this over. He was obviously worried about all these goods on a boat that would sail away leaving an unpaid bill behind.

"Y'all ain't shrimpers, are you?" he asked.

"No, we're the delivery crew for this king crabber. She's got nothing to do with shrimping. We're taking her to Seattle on the West Coast," said Dean, clearly annoyed.

"Oh," answered Roy. His concern about payment intensified.

"Say," said Dean, becoming more frustrated as the woman had no cart. "You wouldn't happen to have another cart. This one's full and we need bedding and sheets."

"Excuse me," said Roy, "but how are y'all goin' to pay for this merchandise?"

"Cash," said the captain, "but I need a receipt for everything. Make it out to Westgate. That's the company we work for. They own the boat."

"OK," said Roy, obviously relieved, "but we'll have to itemize all this merchandise. Betty, you get another cart." She left again, still mumbling under her breath.

Our extended conversation by the cart piled high with kitchenware roused the curiosity of other shoppers. We'd become an attraction. Meanwhile, Henry, still concerned about fully equipping the galley, kept adding items to the mountain in the cart.

"Dean," said Henry in his calm way, "we're going to need a couple of pots bigger than anything I've seen here."

"We can order y'all some larger ones from the catalog," offered Roy, who had begun to recognize a big sales day.

"How long will they take to get here?" asked Dean.

"Hmm, I reckon about a week to ten days," said Roy.

"Too long," snapped the captain. "We've got to get the boat out of here before then."

Betty returned with an empty cart.

"Now we can get started again. We gotta pick out dishes. What kind of patterns you got, Roy?" asked Dean.

Roy was still trying to solve the big pot problem, and dish pattern question jarred him visibly. "Dish patterns?" he said. "Ah, y'all better follow Betty over to the dishware section."

Dean stood in front of the array of dishes for a long time.

"You haven't got anything more nautical, have you? You know, with sailing ships on them?" he asked.

"Oh my, I sure don't think so," said Betty.

"Tough choice. This has got to be something the boat can live with. See anything here that Christine would like?" Dean directed this last question to Henry as he caught up to us. He shook his head no. Dean paced in front of the dishes.

"Who's Christine?" I asked Henry quietly.

"His wife," Henry answered. "She's from the Philippines. She has very definite ideas when it comes to decorating and patterns."

"Oh hell," said Dean. "Damn. I guess we'll take this plain stuff here. Give us a setting of eight—no, make it ten. Maybe they'll have guests on board up north. Boy, what do you think Henry? Will this do?" Dean was in a frenzy over the dish pattern

"Yeah," said Henry calmly, "that ought to do fine. Besides, Christine will like it, too."

"Do you think so?" said Dean inspecting a plate closely. "I sure hope so. OK, let's head for the sheets and bedding. Where is that department?" he asked Roy, who had come up behind us.

"Just over yonder," said Roy, pointing, "but y'all can't go there with this cart."

"What? Why not?" asked Dean looking exasperated, the sweat creating dark circles under his armpits.

"Oh, that's a different department. We have to total all this merchandise right here."

"You mean we've got to go through all this again over there. We can't even take this cart?" He began to wave his arms so that the ash flew off his cigarette.

"That's right, but I'll go with you and introduce you to Billy. He's the manager in that department. Now Betty, you start writing all this up on your sales pad."

Betty produced a sales pad and began writing with painful slowness. Once she had written an item down, she moved the item from the full cart to an empty one. The whole time she kept mumbling, "Oh my, oh my."

"That's going to take a long time. Haven't you got a till where you can just ring up the stuff?" Dean asked.

"Not if y'all need an itemized receipt," answered Roy, walking off toward the linens and bedding.

"Come on, men," said the captain. We followed Roy in a kind of procession. The little crowd of onlookers began to dissipate.

"Say, Dean," said Henry, "Think I'll head downstairs to get tools for the engine room."

"Yeah, go ahead. The boys and I will get the bedding," said Dean.

Billy got the same explanation as Roy and Betty had. Two major problems confronted Dean in this section: choice of sheets and lack of heavy woolen blankets. The first problem related to the color and pattern of sheets for the captain's stateroom. The crew got white sheets, but Dean worked himself into a froth about the color and pattern for his bunk. He examined first one colored set and then another, tending always toward garish colors.

"These have got to look good," he mumbled half to himself. "Christ, you'd think they'd carry something with a little pizazz. Hey, Billy, these all the sheets you got?" He didn't wait for an answer. Finally, through the tobacco smoke and ash, which Billy watched fall onto the sheets, Dean picked a deep purple set. He wanted something with a pattern, he said, but could not find it.

By the time we had heaped two carts full of bedding and towels, the store manager appeared. Dean told the *Scottie* story yet again. Once the store manager confirmed we would pay in cash, he too become sympathetic to our needs, even though, like the others, he had no idea what a king crab boat was and cared little how cold the nights could be on the Bering Sea.

"Sure you don't have some heavy woolen blankets?" Dean asked the store manager.

"No, I sure am sorry, Captain," said the store manager, "We just don't get the demand here in Mobile for woolen blankets!" He laughed at his own little joke. Billy and Roy laughed when the manager did.

"Can you deliver this stuff to Bender Shipyard?" asked Dean who was still impatient and even more wild-eyed after the stress of the sheet decision. "When can we have it on the boat?"

"After we tally it all, to ship it will take several more days," said the manager.

"Hmm, these two boys will pick up the stuff here tomorrow," said Dean

The store manager shrugged, "As you wish, Captain."

From the corner of my eye, I could see Jack's eyebrows go up. How were we going to pick the stuff up? Neither of us, however, wanted more of a scene. After an instant's pause, we nodded in agreement.

Following his last exchange with the manager, Dean led us down to the hardware section where mercifully Henry had just finished selecting the biggest set of mechanics tools Sears had, plus an array of massive wrenches.

"Jesus," said Dean, "I've never been so damn hot in a store. These guys just don't have the stuff we do in Seattle, plus they're slow. They just don't have their act together, right, men?" The captain was oblivious to the irony in this last question. Again, we had no choice but to nod in agreement. Henry looked straight at us. He seemed to be saying, "You see, it is not so easy. The captain is a manipulator," but the look passed in an instant. Instead, he said, "Some items I can't get here. The permanent crew will just have to pick them up in Seattle. This tool set should get us there if nothing major breaks." His last comment hung in the air like a prophecy.

"Let's get the hell out of here," said the captain, storming off but checking over his shoulder to ensure that we followed.

"Hmm," said Henry, "Dean sure is impatient lately."

Back we went to the Admiral Semmes. Dean said he would arrange the food stores via phone. He and Henry would make a few more stops.

"Should we meet tomorrow?" asked Jack as we got out of the car. He wanted to avoid the interminable wait by the phone.

"We'll call you this evening with instructions," said Dean, motioning Henry back into the car. The passenger door slammed, and the Cougar screeched away.

It rained steadily in Mobile that night. We could not walk far without getting soaked, so we ate in the Admiral Semmes. Back in our room, the dank cold had returned. The heating unit, turned up to "High," blew a tepid humidity into the room.

"I just can't get over that scene today," Jack said. "It was a happening. Planning is not the captain's forte."

"That tends to be the way with many Alaskan fishermen, although I've never seen a case like this one. I must admit I've never commissioned a new vessel before."

"At least we could have contacted the store management first and gotten things coordinated," said Jack, lying on his back with his hands behind his head. "Then we could have avoided the repeat scenes in each department."

The phone rang. Jack grabbed the receiver.

"Yes, yes, OK, 9 a.m., but how should we get there? Yes, we'll call a cab. No, that's OK. We're fine here. OK, see you tomorrow." Jack thoughtfully replaced the receiver.

"We're to report on board the *Scottie* tomorrow at 9:00 in the morning. We take a cab to get there. They'll meet us sometime for more provisioning work."

"What about the stuff at Sears?"

"Don't know," said Jack, lying again on his back, hands behind his head. "Guess we'll find out tomorrow."

After the watchman waved us through the gate, the cab dropped us in front of the office. No one was there, so we walked to the *Scottie*. The yard was empty. No work was being done between Christmas and New Year's. We climbed carefully down the rickety dock ladder and dropped onto the aft deck. The deck door was not locked. Inside, we called out, but the boat was deserted. We sat at the galley table.

"Oh-nine-hundred hours and no sign of the skipper and engineer," I commented, half to myself.

"No sign of life in the yard either," said Jack.

Being on the boat, however, gave us hope that soon the engine below would be powering us though the aquamarine Caribbean.

"Sure would be great to be on our way," I said.

"Yeah, at least we've started outfitting the boat," said Jack. "I'm looking forward to being in our cabin. The Admiral Semmes is getting on my nerves."

"I wonder how she handles at sea. She sure is beamy and the Cat engine down below looks like it will push us along at a good pace."

Just then we heard an engine and the sound of tires rattling across the planking of the dock. A door slammed. Jack stood, craning to get a look up at the dock through a galley porthole.

"Hey, y'all down there on the *Scottie*, I got your delivery."

"It's a truck," said Jack as we stepped out onto the aft deck. A burly truck driver stared down at us.

"I got your hooch. You'd better get on up here to help me unload," he said.

"Hooch?" asked Jack

"Yup," said the trucker, "Forty-eight cases of beer and four of hard liquor. Your captain said y'all was goin' to Alaska and this should hold you to the Panama!" he laughed. "Come on up now, I got to get goin'."

"Holy shit," said Jack as we scrambled up the ladder.

The truck had been backed onto the dock, which surprisingly had not collapsed under the weight. The big-bellied driver wrestled open the back gate, and we unloaded the cases. The hard liquor was mainly Scotch, with a couple bottles of gin thrown into one open box. The beer made an impressive stack on the dock.

"One thing for sure, you boys from Alaska pack a powerful thirst," said the driver. "And I thought some of the shrimpers here could drink!"

He made us sign a delivery slip, then hoisted himself back into the cab. The truck rumbled away with the dock's plank ends working up and down like keys on a player piano. Suddenly, the truck stopped. The driver's head popped from his side window.

"Y'all put the beer in the forepeak and the hard stuff in the captain's cabin. Them's the orders from your captain." The head disappeared into the truck as it lurched away.

The tide in the muddy arm of Mobile Bay was high enough that we could hand the cases of beer and liquor from the dock to the deck. Even so, each case had a short free-fall when Jack released it before I caught it. We worked with a will, not knowing what the tide would do next. Our first goal was to move all the cases from the dock onto the deck, which we accomplished in about an hour of steady work.

Stowing the four cases of liquor in the captain's cabin required but a few minutes. Stowing the forty-eight cases of beer in the forepeak was another matter. From the aft deck, we stepped over the high sill of the watertight door; descended the steep ladder to the engine room; transited the tight passage on the port side between the Caterpillar engine and the piping, valves, and electrical cable trays; climbed the steps forward of the engine; stepped through a watertight bulkhead door; and stacked each case in the small space of the forepeak. The forty-eight cases of beer filled the space and would be handy to the workbench where a thirsty engineer could pause a moment to sip a brew.

At first, I was stationed in the forepeak for stacking while Jack hauled in each case. After three trips, the sweat poured off Jack while I languished before the arrival of the next case. Then we each carried a case and stacked it ourselves. Each trip was a steeplechase combining high stepping through the watertight doors, the frightful decent down the steel ladder (its steps could not be seen over a case of beer in one's arms), twisting sideways to walk through the engine room, ascending the narrow steps up to the forepeak level, passing through its watertight door and stacking the case. After a few trips, we stopped on the aft deck, sweat dripping off our faces.

"When do we lie on the deck chairs?" I asked Jack, who was draped over a stack of beer cases.

"That reminds me, we have to get a couple of deck chairs," he said.

"I find it a bit ironic that the first thing we load on this boat is a mountain of beer and enough Scotch for a fifth a day clear to Seattle," I observed.

"I hope Dean isn't too heavy into the sauce to get us from Mobile to Panama," said Jack, hoisting another case and heading for the high hurdle at the watertight door.

Up and down we went. We were careful to keep the stack low while interlocking the cases so they would not fly about in heavy seas. Despite our occasional grumbling about the officer's alcohol capacity, we preferred the work to staring at the blank walls of the Admiral Semmes' dismal room.

Noon arrived. Having just packed the last case below, we sat on the main hatch. The sun broke though the overcast for the first time since we arrived. Ferocious in its warmth, such intensity did not arrive in our northern latitudes until well into summer. The breeze felt good. We could see a shrimper not far off with a cloud of raucous gulls trailing behind. Two deck hands were picking through a mound of shrimp flinging trash fish and debris over the side. The gulls twisted, wheeled, and dove in combat flight to grab the scraps. Sunlight glinted from their white wings. So absorbed were we in the gull's animated flight that we failed to hear the approach of the Cougar until she was above us dockside.

"How's it going, men?" Dean asked as his feet hit the deck.

"Here," yelled Henry, dropping down two paper bags, one at a time.

"Did you get any deliveries?" Dean asked.

"Yes," answered Jack, with a hint of disdain that at least I could detect. "The four cases of hard stuff are in your stateroom. The forty-eight cases of beer are stowed in the forepeak."

"Great," said the captain, so elated to have the shipment on board that he did not notice the tone of Jack's voice. "We won't be thirsty on the trip, then. You know you go through a lot of body fluids in the tropics so that beer is important."

"Probably would be good to order some soft drinks, too," added Henry, landing on deck from the ladder with a solid thump.

"Might be good to have juice for the mornings," I offered, hiding my desperation at the thought of beer for breakfast.

"Oh, yeah, sure—that stuff is coming, but I'll up the juice order now that you mention it," said Dean.

"OK, Henry and I will take a lunch break. You two head for Sears and pick up that stuff. Here's the keys to the car. Let's see, here's three hundred bucks—that ought to cover it. Grab yourselves some lunch out of that and bring me back all the receipts." Dean tossed the car keys to me. He and Henry seated themselves on the hatch, plunging their hands into the bags and pulling out hamburgers.

Jack and I scrambled up the dock ladder and jumped into the car.

"I wonder if Dean realized how much work it was to get the beer below. The most work they did was loading their hamburgers onboard," grumbled Jack.

"Yeah, for a minute I thought they had brought us lunch, but no such luck," I said. "Well, at least we have the car and can get a bite of our own."

"That's what we'll do first!" said Jack.

I wheeled the Cougar out of the deserted yard toward downtown. We found a hamburger joint for lunch and gobbled down burgers that oozed grease through the buns. After a wandering course, we located the Sears Roebuck store.

"How are we going to get all that stuff is this car?" I asked Jack as I switched off the ignition.

Within, we found Roy, who directed us to the loading dock "out back." We drove around. A guy on the loading dock gave the Cougar a long look.

"Befo' y'all begin, you better go inside and pay." We did so, paying the girl at the Will Call window, who never said a word during the transaction.

Back on the loading dock, the guy had a question for us.

"Don't y'all have a pick-up? 'Cause you gonna have a helluva time loading this heap of stuff in that rig." He had us sign off on the paperwork, then walked away, waving his hand in the direction of our pile of goods.

Taking items from the cardboard shipping boxes and wedging them into every nook and cranny, we packed the Cougar's trunk, which had the cargo area of a large handbag. We used the same method in the back seat, but halfway through we realized that one large box would only fit in the front passenger seat. We gained considerably by leaving one small space for me in the back and filling the rest of the front passenger space to the ceiling. Jack, being the taller of the two of us, drove. I wedged myself into the tiny space in the back seat and Jack placed a last box on my lap.

From the driver's seat, Jack could see ahead and to the left but not at all to the right. He could only see behind from the driver's side rear-view mirror. With the large box on my lap and goods all around, I could only see out the small rear window on the right side. Neither of us had ever been in a tank, but rolling out of the parking lot, communicating what we could see from our separate vantage points, we had the distinct impression that we were in one.

Only a generous police lunch hour could explain how we were not arrested on the drive back to the yard. Numbness replaced normal feeling in my right leg. A large cardboard carton protruding over the back of the driver's seat forced Jack to drive leaning forward with head held erect to see out the front window. Somehow, we made it. In the first seconds out of the car, Jack stood, eyes skyward, massaging the back of his neck to return blood to knotted muscles.

As we boarded with the first armloads of Sears goods, we thought the *Scottie* was empty, but the captain and engineer were in the engine room. Whatever their mission, it had led them to the forepeak and provided each with a can of the recently stowed beer.

"Hey, you're finally back," said the captain with a jovial wave of the beer can, "What took so long?"

"The Cougar wasn't easy to load, and we didn't want to leave things on the loading dock while making a second trip," I said. "We've got it all now. Here's the receipts from Sears and lunch."

"OK. Get the stuff on board. As soon as Henry and I finish here, we'll be up to give you a hand stowing that crap."

Whatever their mission in the engine room, it consumed a great deal of time. Jack and I had unloaded the car and lowered the goods, including the heavy tools, down to the deck. Dean appeared just as we lowered the last of the heavy tools, which gave him the idea that we should move the tools to the engine room while he tackled such back-breaking items as sheets and pillows. Henry stationed himself at the tool bench in the engine room, directing us where to place each heavy load. He did the same in the galley. Jack and I hauled in armloads of cooking utensils while he fussed about, organizing the storage. His enthusiasm for stowing the galley items eclipsed that of the tools' storage. The entire time he worked, he recounted his favorite recipes, raising expectations of gourmet meals as we steamed over azure seas.

The captain remained locked away in his stateroom. As we finished in the galley, he emerged triumphantly, inviting us in. He had made the bed with the purple sheets. Proudly, he showed us the organization of drawers for bath linens. He pointed out that he'd carefully coordinated colors and patterns. Henry nodded approval of the captain's domestic capacities. Jack and I, not knowing what to say, followed Henry's lead, nodding and expressing a true amazement at his mastery of patterns and colors.

Later Jack and I made up our own bunks and laid out a towel each. This simple act seemed to improve our chances for actually departing Mobile. When we left the yard, however, it remained as empty as it had all week. In his late-night phone calls to Cindy, Jack complained about the inactivity at the yard. The message must have gotten through. The next day, when we arrived at the ship after buying charts and navigational items, the yard was alive. The foreman's greeting was curt.

The trip to the ship chandlery to buy charts and navigation equipment had been as disconcerting as the assault on Sears. In addition to a complete set of charts along the track of the voyage, the captain bought many charts that barely abutted the course. Were these for forays into foreign ports or in case *Scottie* was off course? To the charts, the captain added all the coastal pilots, navigational texts, and guides that the store offered. He had an obsession for time/distance wheels. He purchased at least two plotters, dividers, and triangles, plus an exquisite marine clock and barometer. He ordered the flag of every country we would pass along the route.

At the yard, workers were bustling about on the *Scottie*. Jack and I were storing the navigational equipment with the captain supervising when the foreman arrived.

"Shakedown cruise tomorrow, captain," he announced ceremoniously.

"Good," Jack whispered in my ear.

"Yes, sir," carried on the foreman, "we'll be ready at 08:00 hours tomorrow morning. We'll also have the man here to swing the compass."

"We'll be ready," responded the captain, in his own official tone. "We've got orders from Westgate to put the boat through her paces, you know."

"Y'all will find this here vessel ship shape. She'll take anything y'all can throw at her," answered the foreman with bravado.

CHAPTER VII
SEA TRIALS

The cab dropped us at the yard at 7:45 a.m. Walking down the dock, we heard *Scottie*'s main engine idling, a confident deep rumble. On the bridge, a yard worker chatted with the man who would swing the compass. No captain or engineer. Jack and I checked the engine room. No sign of Dean or Henry there either. Even at idle, the big Caterpillar diesel had already warmed the engine room space.

Back on the bridge, the compass adjuster had the binnacle open, and a yard worker was checking wiring under the main instrument panel. The foreman was pontificating to a cohort.

"Y'all ready for a little cruise?" bellowed the foreman when he spied us coming up the companionway. "She's warmed up and rarin' to go. Ain't that right, Del?"

"Sho' enough. Got a fine boat here," said Del, not missing his cue.

"Where's the captain?" asked the foreman.

"He should be along any minute," I answered, "but he and the engineer stay at a different hotel than we do."

"Well, that's the way it is with captains and chief engineers," said the foreman, "they always get a better deal than the crew."

Jack and I left the bridge, making our way to the aft deck to sit on the hatch combing looking out toward Mobile Bay. A good breeze blew in from the sea. Puffy white clouds dappled the water, casting shadows intermixed with brilliant shafts of sunlight.

At 8:00 a.m., Jack turned to me and said, "You don't suppose the captain and engineer will be late for sea trials? I knew it; I just knew it, but I'm still hoping this won't happen. We haven't seen the captain and engineer before noon since we got to Mobile."

At 8:30, the foreman waddled out of the deck house.

"Where's that skipper of yours?" He was loud enough for half the yard to hear.

"Don't know," Jack responded, mustering a cheerful firmness in his tone of voice. The foreman shrugged and huffed back into the galley. Neither Jack nor I moved, wanting to avoid any further questions. We fully understood that, although we saw ourselves as independent from the captain and engineer, the yard identified us as captain and crew—the foreigners who forced them to work during the Christmas break. Whatever the actions of the captain and engineer, we would be tarred with the same brush. Now the boat was ready, and we were not.

At 9:30, the Cougar rolled up on the land end of the dock. The captain and engineer tumbled out, walked along the dock, and descended the ladder. Jack and I crossed the deck to alert them of the foreman's mood, but the man bolted from the deck house before we could say anything.

"Ah, there y'all are. We've been ready for nearly two hours," he announced to the world. As Dean turned from the ladder to face the foreman, it was painfully obvious that he was in no shape for this confrontation. His usually pale complexion was pasty, his countenance puffy. The bags under his bloodshot eyes were enormous. An unlit cigarette was pasted to his dry lower lip. His shirt and pants exhibited the chaos of wrinkles only achieved by sleeping in them. The black dress loafers were sadly inappropriate on a commercial fishing boat. The man was a garish neon sign advertising a pulsating hangover.

"Well, we're ready to put her through her paces," Dean said, but the words were hollow. "Henry, check out the engine room."

The foreman had the high ground but couldn't push his advantage further as Dean slipped past with Henry close behind. They headed into the deck house. Henry descended the engine room ladder and remained below for the trials. The foreman followed the captain to the bridge. Jack and I brought up the rear.

On the bridge, I noticed a stale alcoholic odor emanating from the captain. The foreman explained the function and operation of the vessel's controls in a loud voice that left Dean wincing. While the foreman continued his non-stop monologue, Dean fumbled to light the cigarette dangling from his lip. The tobacco fortified him long enough to allow him to deftly suggest that the foreman "take her out." Jack and I were ordered to the deck to help the yard workers cast off the lines.

The sun broke through the scudding clouds just as *Scottie* backed away from the dock. The propeller wash churned the water behind the stern. Soon the wake formed rolling waves. *Scottie* sallied forth into Mobile Bay in a brisk wind that built a short breaking chop. Gulls followed us, wheeling and crying. At last underway, our spirits soared with the gulls. The shake-down cruise banished our memory of the days of endless delay. Not knowing what else was expected of us, we hung about on the deck enjoying the open air and the wake rolling in a widening "V" astern. Finally, we made our way back to the bridge.

The bridge was silent. Dean had found the captain's chair. He sat in its soft leather, slumped down, his head propped up by his arm with his elbow planted on the chair's arm rest. The foreman stood before the wheel steering *Scottie* between the long line of buoys leading seaward. The compass adjuster stood on the port side of the bridge beside the open sliding window, apparently enjoying the view. The short wind-driven chop on the bay transmitted a lurching motion that rocked the slumped captain back and forth like gelatin.

"Well, what do y'all say about the *Scottie* now?" bellowed the foreman as soon as he noted our ascent to the bridge.

"She seems just fine," I answered.

"One hell of a boat," the foreman continued. "She moves right nice, wouldn't you say, Captain?"

"Uh huh," said Dean, unable to lift his head from his hand.

"We'll run out further 'till we get ourselves some sea room, then you can take over, Skipper, for the trials," said the foreman, smiling.

"Good," said Dean in the economical monotone of endurance.

"We'll have a look in the engine room," Jack announced.

"OK," Dean roused from his stupor. "Let me know how Henry's doing."

Jack and I quickly left the bridge, went back through the main passage and the galley, then descended the steep steel ladder into the engine room. Noise and heat roiled up to greet us. The diesel main was thumping away, muscling the 90-foot-long hull though the sea. We made our way around the white mass of engine, finding Henry and a man from the yard standing before a complex array of valves mounted on the engine room's aft starboard bulkhead. The fellow was pointing at valves, then yelling explanations into Henry's ear. Sweat beaded Henry's brow and dripped from his nose. The valves controlled the flow of seawater into *Scottie*'s two cavernous live tanks. The king crab, after being hauled from deep in the sea in big pots, were kept alive in these recirculating seawater tanks until the vessel unloaded them for processing. The tanks took up most of the hull under the aft deck, with the exception of the lazarette at the stern. When both tanks were full, *Scottie*, like all king crabbers, sat low in the water, or "half sunk" in the vernacular of the king crab fishermen. While the yard worker yelled and motioned instructions, Henry stood immobile. As we approached, I wondered if the valve lesson was sinking in.

"The captain asks how things are going?" I yelled.

"Fine," said Henry.

Needing no greater excuse than Henry's terse response to leave the hot engine room, we returned to the bridge. Dean had dozed off in the captain's chair but roused to a full sitting position as we noisily topped the final steps.

"What's the report from the engine room?" asked Dean, peering ahead at the bay with its muddy waves and low adjoining lands.

"All is fine, according to Henry," answered Jack.

"Well, I told y'all. You got one hell of a vessel here," said the foreman. "You can take her now, Captain."

Dean struggled to his feet, lurching to the wheel as the foreman stepped aside.

"Go down and tell Henry that we're starting the trials," Dean ordered Jack, who left again for the engine room.

Dean steadied himself at the helm, then studied the controls and dials on the console. He reached for the red-handled throttle and slowed the boat down, then turned her to starboard. The boat responded immediately. Jack was back on the bridge by the time the captain swung the boat to port. Dean peered aft through the stern-facing bridge windows to ensure no traffic was behind, then eased the gear lever from forward through neutral to reverse.

The propeller churned water forward, which roiled out on either side of the hull. As the *Scottie* backed, the choppy waves smacked the stern, showering fine spray over the aft deck.

Dean eased the gear lever from astern through neutral to forward. He then pushed the throttle forward, bringing the king crabber up to cruising speed, which he held momentarily. He cut an odd figure, standing before the wheel in his wrinkled clothes and black dress loafers. A bead of sweat trickled down his face. He spun the wheel to starboard. Everyone hung on as the vessel careened in the hard turn. Deep into the turn, Dean shoved the throttle full forward. Dark smoke rolled out of the smokestack as the diesel dug in. *Scottie* accelerated through the turn and Dean spun the helm, bringing the boat to a straight course. The hull speed increased, and the wake rolled from the stern in deep waves. The captain then pulled the throttle back. Before the speeding hull could slow, he pulled the gear lever from forward into reverse. The vessel shuddered in reverse, then the throttle was pushed forward, and the prop wash boiled forward. The foreman looked concerned, but the boat withstood the maneuver. I wondered what it sounded and felt like down in the engine room. The captain eased the throttle back again and put the engine into neutral.

"She'll hold together," he announced. He stepped back, indicating to the foreman that the helm was his. This caught the foreman by surprise. Dean crawled up into the captain's chair again, his face deathly white. Sweat rolled down from his temple while semi-circles of sweat radiated from under each arm. He lit another cigarette and inhaled deeply.

The foreman announced to the compass adjuster that he would take *Scottie* to "the range" for swinging the compass.

"You boys check on Henry," said the captain after another deep drag. Jack and I descended from the bridge.

"Was that it?" Jack asked as we turned from the main passageway into the galley.

"Maybe so," I answered. "I've never been on a sea trial before. Doesn't seem as though he wants to do much today."

"He's so hungover he couldn't do much even if he wanted!" said Jack. "A lot of systems haven't been tried, like most of the navigation equipment, the radar, radios—all that stuff."

The engine room was no louder but felt definitely hotter after the maneuvers. Henry and the yard man were at the work bench. The yard worker was still yelling explanations, pointing and gesticulating while Henry was quiet and sweating.

"No major problems," was his answer. He requested a beer from the refrigerator.

Jack went to the bridge while I fetched cold beers for Henry and the yard man. When I handed then over, they were snatched away, pull tabs ripped open and bottoms tilted toward the upper decks.

"It's damn important to keep fluid in the body in these southern climates," Henry yelled to me over the engine noise, "We gotta remember to buy salt tablets."

I stayed in the engine room despite the heat. The yard worker talked to Henry about operating the auxiliary generators. I wondered in the noise and heat if this was the best way to transfer information about the boat's multiple systems. I headed back to the bridge.

Once up the ladder from the engine room, I turned aft and shoved open the watertight door to the aft deck. I pushed it open all the way, securing it with a hook on the back of the deck house. The air felt fresh and cool. A few gulls chased us. The symphony of the wake accompanied the vessel's progress. The sun broke through, splashing color over the seascape. If only we did not have to return to the confusion and delays of the land.

On the bridge, the captain slept with head tilted back on the captain's chair, his mouth open. He snored. The foreman was gone. The compass adjuster was at the helm. Jack gazed out the open side window. I made my way quietly across the bridge to Jack.

"Where's the foreman?" I asked.

"Down in the engine room. Didn't you see him?"

"No, I was on the aft deck for a few minutes. Looks like the boat put the skipper through his paces, not vice-versa."

Just then the compass adjuster slowed the boat. The change in engine speed brought the captain upright, bubbling and snorting.

"Huh, oh, must have dozed off for a second," said Dean half to himself and half to the man at the helm.

"I'm on the range now and will be maneuvering back and forth a trifle to swing the compass."

"Good, good, carry on," said Dean. He climbed down from his chair and went below.

Jack and I chatted with the compass adjuster as he lined *Scottie* up first with one landmark then another, adjusting the small magnetic bars around the compass and making notations on the little compass deviation card. When finished, he set the card in a small wooden frame mounting it in plain view above the binnacle. With this ritual complete, *Scottie* joined vessels large and small that could, with an accurate chronometer and a sextant, find her way across trackless seas.

The foreman reappeared and took the *Scottie* back to her berth. Dean, having slept through the return voyage, did not accept the offer to dock the boat. Jack and I secured the lines dockside. The foreman with his yard crew left the boat as soon as Henry received his last instruction, how to shut the main engine down. Long past quitting time, the yard was silent. Dean and Henry compared a few notes, then the captain declared his ravenous hunger. Despite Henry's desire to check one more thing, the captain shanghaied him, and they were soon roaring away in the Cougar.

Jack and I were in no hurry to depart. Behind broken clouds, the sun set. The wind had turned damp, but the day had given us a taste of the real voyage, with the land slipping astern, leaving the clear dominion of the sea. Eventually we caught a cab back to the motel. That night, the Admiral Semmes echoed like a prison.

❋

Although we moved our gear onto the boat the following day, the *Scottie* was not yet ready to depart. The shake-down cruise shook down the captain's status more than anything else. The foreman had triumphed and the list of items remaining to be completed languished.

The delays of the land returned. The day following the sea trials— Tuesday, December 30, 1969—passed in complete inactivity. No one, of course, worked on New Year's Eve. The captain magnanimously declared that the holiday was to be strictly observed, a pronouncement that thinly masked his self-indulgence. Only Jack and I wished to be away, to carry on with the voyage instead of celebrating.

For New Year's Eve in Mobile, we did not attempt to link up with the captain and engineer, as we had long since learned that their tastes and cash flow differed markedly from ours. We decided to find our own merriment.

At a cafe, we asked the waitress where the young people went on New Year's Eve. She gave us the name of a ballroom on the outskirts of the town. At 9:30 p.m. we called a cab, giving the driver the name of the place. We sat in the back of the cab conjecturing about how late we could return to school, assuming a departure right after New Year's Day.

The conversation diverted our attention. The cab drove on and on. Suddenly, Jack, who had the directions to the ballroom written down, noticed a sign.

"Hey, where are you going?" he asked the man at the wheel.

"Pardon, suh?" asked the cabbie.

"Where are you taking us?" said Jack loudly.

"To the ballroom, suh," he answered, but stared narrow-eyed at Jack in the rearview mirror.

"No, you aren't!" said Jack, "But you better start now and turn off that meter because we've passed the place and you know it."

"This is the fastest way," protested the cabbie who, nevertheless, reached over and shut off the meter.

A few minutes later, the cabbie exited the freeway, then wound along secondary lanes for several miles, turning at last into a parking lot beside a large building. I paid the outrageous $18 fare.

"Damn," I said to Jack, "New Year's Eve and the cabbies are out to make a killing. He marked us as foreigners before we got into the cab!"

"Well, we're here," said Jack. "Let's make the best of it."

The parking lot was dimly lit. The building gave the impression of being a huge Quonset hut. As we approached the entrance, the door burst open, and three boys dressed in tuxedoes staggered out. In the instant the door was open, we clearly heard a band playing and glimpsed a big crowd. Balloons floated up toward the dark, domed ceiling.

The sound of retching distracted us from further consideration of the interior. One of the boys was projectile vomiting onto the side of the build- ing: it ricocheted onto his tux. His two companions were dutifully support- ing his slumping frame. Jack and I turned simultaneously, but the cab had already departed. We paid the cover charge and entered.

We did not consider ourselves old, but the crowd inside, all in formal dress, appeared dominated by high schoolers. The girls stood in tight groups gig- gling while the boys careened about being loud, truculent, and drunk. The band played big band tunes, but now and then mixed in rock and roll from the late 1950s, which brought the crowd screaming and careening onto the dance floor. Beer was everywhere. It formed an insidiously spreading lake on the floor. Several semi-conscious boys slumped over tables and chairs.

Although we spoke the same language, we could not communicate with these natives. The heavy Southern accent, slurred by alcohol, left conversation garbled, but even if it had not been so, we knew nothing of local football. We dressed differently. Soon we turned to the doorman and requested a cab. One arrived within ten minutes. Although the ride out took 45 minutes, we were back at the Admiral Semmes in 15 minutes, an hour before midnight.

The prospect of being in our dismal hotel room at the beginning of the new decade forced us out. We wandered toward the harbor. We found a little bar with a festive atmosphere created in large part by a Scottish tanker crew. We had no trouble understanding them through their sometimes thick brogue. Our conversation touched on all manner of worldly events. At midnight, we all sang "Auld Lang Syne."

New Year's Day slid by marked by a late morning and a numbing string of bowl games on television blending one into another. Jack called Cindy. Bill had decided to fly to Mobile and was scheduled to arrive the following afternoon, to make sure *Scottie* finally got underway. He had again been guaranteed by the yard that the vessel would be ready to go.

I called home. My mother sounded tired. My parents had divorced years ago, leaving her to raise four children on a registered nurse's income. She was always in favor of risks and adventures, so had encouraged this voyage. Earning money was frosting on the cake. Yet I was the last to leave home and the thought of her being alone on New Year's Day left guilt lingering over the rest of the doleful day.

The malaise of New Year's Day evaporated in the sunlit, exuberant air of the next morning. It was Friday, January 2, 1970, the day we were to check out of the Semmes and sail into the Caribbean. As the doors of the Admiral Semmes closed behind us, we were ending the long, sour chapter of perpetual delays. On board the boat, we neatly stowed the last of our gear while yard workers bustled about with checklists in hand. By the uncharacteristically early hour of 10:00 a.m., the captain and engineer brought the last of their gear on board. Departure resonated through the boat.

CHAPTER VIII
DEPARTURE

Suddenly a man, some kind of agent to somebody, appeared with full powers.

—Joseph Conrad, *Youth*

To our delight, Bill arrived on board at 1:30 in the afternoon. We'd all gathered around the main hatch to discuss the voyage. Jack and I were ready. Bill was ready to send us on our way. The foreman was anxious to finally be rid of us. The captain was ready. Henry was not going anywhere.

"I am not sailing on a Friday in a new boat," he said this quietly but with stubborn determination. Bill, who was a large man, was walking toward the deck house door to inspect the *Scottie*'s interior and the pronouncement stopped him in his tracks.

"What?" he asked, slowly turning to look at Henry.

"You know it's bad luck sailing on a Friday and worse yet in a new boat. This is really asking for trouble," said Henry.

Bill studied the face of the short, rotund engineer. He said nothing for a long while but looked the engineer right in the eye. Neither blinked. The captain stood by the hatch, and for once he did not fidget. Jack stood, his eyebrows raised. He could not believe his ears. I must have looked the same. How in this modern era, with a steel-hulled, diesel-driven vessel packed with the latest electronics, could the engineer, a man of the world, be talking seriously about seafaring superstition to his boss? The tension resonated between the two men.

"All right," said Bill, slowly, "maybe you've got a point there." He glanced at Jack and me, then studied the captain. "Maybe we shouldn't push our luck. You'll sail tomorrow, early. Now let's have a look around." He turned and headed through the galley door.

The captain breathed a sigh of relief. Henry said, half to himself and half to the back of the businessman who was stepping over the threshold of the watertight door, "Thanks." Then he followed, as did the captain.

"Can you believe that?" asked Jack, incredulously. "Who would have thought Henry the superstitious type. I can't believe Bill agreed to hold us another day for a superstition."

"Well," I said, "I guess we're in Mobile another night after all." Though disappointed, I was amazed that seafaring myths still ran deep, could be spoken out loud, and were respected.

"Aren't you coming?" asked Jack, as he walked toward the deck door. "At least we better follow along and keep listening. No telling what might pop up next."

Bill wanted to see everything on the *Scottie*. He had a quick eye, taking in all the boat's features at a glance. In the engine room, he noticed immediately that the lube oil day tanks were only partly filled. The diesel main pumped oil from one day tank through the engine into a second day tank. These were mounted on the engine room bulkheads, one on each side of the engine. At the start of a long voyage at least one day tank should be full. According to the sight glasses, which Henry should have noticed, neither was.

"Get the foreman," said Bill curtly.

When he arrived, the foreman was momentarily at a loss for words. Henry was apologetic. According to the watch on the foreman's wrist, it was 3:30 and the fuel dock, where lube oil could be purchased in quantity, closed at 4:00 sharp—not enough time to move the boat there. Further, the fuel dock would not re-open until Monday morning.

"We're not losing another weekend," said Bill to the foreman. "We've got to get this show moving. You get me four drums of lube oil on this boat today. Order them from the fuel dock now and have them delivered here by truck."

The drums arrived dockside at 4:30. With a generator set running for power, we used one of the crab pot booms, rigged a sling, and lowered the drums onto the deck. Then came the problem of getting the lube oil out of a drum into the day tank in the engine room. Under Bill's direction, Henry rigged a hose from one of the drums, snaked it down the companionway, through the engine room and into the fill spout of the starboard day tank.

Despite the height of the drum up on the deck, the molasses consistency of the lube oil yielded a flow rate that would keep *Scottie* in Mobile for another month.

"Get a sling back on the drum," commanded Bill. Jack and I jumped to it, the fear of days more in Mobile motivating us. The drum was hoisted high above the deck dangling from a crab boom. The extra height had the oil running like maple syrup in spring. The first 55-gallon drum went into the tank, and we started another. It was now nearly 6:00, and Bill said he had to get back to the hotel to make some calls. The captain and engineer had run up quite a bill at the Ramada, which Bill had to settle before they could leave. We caught bits and pieces of this dialogue regarding debts run up here and there around the town. Bill was determined to settle these himself. "No more cash advances," we heard him bark at Dean. Bill said he would be back to pick us up for a "last dinner ashore for a while." Bill, Dean, and Henry drove off with Jack and I left to monitor the lube oil.

"We are going to make it tomorrow," said Jack once we were alone on the boat.

"I thought this lube oil problem had cooked us for yet another weekend. I'm surprised Henry didn't see it. Bill really moved the ball though. If he hadn't been here, *Scottie* would be at the fuel dock on Monday instead of at sea," I noted.

"God, I can't wait to get going," said Jack. "I had a horrible vision of us trapped in Mobile waiting the rest of our lives!"

Dusk faded into night. The sky had become overcast, but the breeze diminished so we stayed on the aft deck watching lights come on along the waterway. The moments we spent looking at the fading day were costly. When we went below, we found that the lube oil had overflowed and was streaming down the outside of the tank in thick streaks pooling on the deck plates. Jack kinked the hose while I ran top side and lowered the drum. In a fit of compelling embarrassment, because we had been so critical of everyone else, we set to work with paper towels swiping up the thick oil. By the time Bill returned, the mess was cleaned up but we had put a serious dent in the paper towel supply. We confessed our error to Bill, who rolled his eyes.

"Henry was right," he said. "It's damn lucky I didn't send you out on a Friday!" which was the only comment he ever made about that sailor's superstition.

We showered quickly and drove with Bill to meet the captain and engineer for dinner. No rancor soured the meal. A round of drinks, thick steaks, baked potatoes with all the trimmings put everyone in a good mood. Stories flowed from Bill and Dean about other new boats and adventures on the sea. At dinner's end, Bill gave his parting words of wisdom: ". . .caution and vigilance, and no more cash draws for the captain."

The farewell dinner and sleeping in our cabin confirmed that we would at last sail in the morning. The water lapped against the hull, a melodious sound drifting in through the open portholes by our bunks. The boat rocked just slightly, bringing the deep sleep that comes only on the water.

LOGBOOK, DAY 1: JANUARY 3, 1970

A generator set started. Henry, perhaps because of his demands and lapses of the day before, was up first. Jack popped out from the lower bunk, grabbed a towel, and headed for the shower. With the sound of the spewing shower came the odd tones of his singing. The main engine grumbled to life and settled into a steady rumbling purr. Dressed in fresh work pants and shirt, I went out on the back deck. The wind was blowing. Clouds blocked most of the sky, but sunlight seared through at their ragged edges. Looking up to the bridge through its stern-facing windows, I could see the captain moving back and forth, turning on the electronics. One radar antenna began to rotate.

Jack joined me, his hair still wet from the shower. It was 08:00 when the yard foreman came swaggering along the dock. Dean stepped from the bridge via its aft facing port side door, the one nearest the dock.

"OK, cut her loose," Dean yelled down to us, "and stow the dock lines and fenders in the hold. We won't see those again until we're in the Panama Canal." Then he addressed the foreman, "We're going to leave you alone now. What are you going to do for fun?"

"Oh, I know I'm gonna be lonely now without y'all to keep me occupied," said the foreman with a big friendly grin, "but I got more like this one to build. Y'all take good care of this fine boat now."

The foreman helped cast off the dock lines. Jack and I pulled them on board with the speed of enthusiastic youth, not the measured pace of the professional. The *Scottie* eased into reverse and kicked her stern smartly away from the dock. We could see Dean spin the wheel to starboard and she nosed her way into the channel. The engine RPM increased, and the wake began to grow as white water churned astern. The gulls soared overhead. The wind freshened as the boat gained way for the Panama Canal.

Jack and I pulled in the tires that served as fenders and coiled the heavy dock lines. We lashed the tires to the aft rail on the port side. We slid back the hatch cover on the forward live tank. Below, a removable steel ladder reached to the bottom of the cavernous tank. We dropped the lines in and I climbed down. When I looked up, Henry and Jack were framed against the sky yelling directions and advice on where and how to stow the lines. I piled the lines forward against the engine room bulkhead. By the time I emerged from the metal dungeon, *Scottie* was well into the long channel leading out of Mobile Bay. Buoys marched toward the horizon marking the channel in the wide expanse of the shallow bay.

"About time for some breakfast, don't you think?" said Henry with a smile. "Guess I'll go whip something up. You wouldn't be opposed to pancakes, would you?" he asked.

"Of course not," responded Jack emphatically.

Leaving Henry bustling about in the galley, Jack and I climbed to the bridge, which hummed with electronics. Both LORAN sets were on, one radar, the non-recording depth finder, and both radios, each on a different channel. The view from the bridge was expansive. The channel was empty of other ships or boats but a mile or so ahead, a dredge was working on one side of the channel. Several of her anchor marker buoys extended to mid-channel. The wind had worried up a short chop on the bay's mud brown waters.

"Well, we're finally on the road," said Dean from behind the wheel, with a sweeping gesture forward. "We'll be in the Panama in five days. What do you say to that?"

"Great," I said. "Damn, it's good to be underway at last."

"Yeah," said Dean, puffing a cigarette, then pulling it away from his mouth expansively between index and middle fingers, "Mobile was getting old, all right."

Scottie closed the distance between herself and the dredge with good speed. Beyond the dredge, we saw a shrimp boat coming in, her outriggers down, which consumed a good bit of sea space considering the narrow width of the channel. The *Scottie* and the shrimper were going to arrive at the dredge at the same time.

"Look at that damn shrimper with her outriggers down, taking up half the channel," said Dean. *Scottie* sped onward.

The shrimper passed nearest to the dredge's mid-channel anchor buoys. *Scottie*, never altering her pace by a single RPM, had to pass wide of the shrimper's port side outrigger, which forced the captain to lay the wheel hard to starboard. *Scottie* veered not only wide of the shrimper's outrigger but also wide of the channel.

"Jesus, he's going to run us aground. Watch that depth finder!" yelled Dean as he fought to turn *Scottie*'s wheel hard to port just as the shrimper passed. The depth finder, which had been indicating a steady forty feet suddenly jumped up to eight feet. "That's it, we're aground!" yelled Dean. He had seen the depth finder jump up but his flailing at the wheel pulled his head away from the view of the finder's screen. *Scottie* yawed hard to starboard turning back toward the channel, her wake a drunken arc.

Jack and I held on through the high-speed turn waiting for the hull to slam into the mud. Despite Dean's yelling that we were aground, the thud never came. Just as suddenly as the depth had leapt upward on the finder's screen, it dropped away again.

"We've made it. We're back in the channel!" shouted Dean with the relief of one reprieved from death row. *Scottie* once again steamed along in mid-channel. I stepped to the bridge's aft facing windows. Dense clouds of mud rolled in our wake where its arc still lingered outside the channel. We had not missed the bottom by much. Just then Henry came up the bridge steps.

"What's the matter?" he asked. He had obviously been hurled from one side of the galley to the other and wondered why the boat was reeling like a drunk.

"That shrimper back there ran us wide of the channel at the dredge anchor buoys," answered Dean. "The boys here saw it," he added cleverly, ensuring our complicit answer. "He damn near put us on that mud bank, didn't he, men?" Jack and I had no choice but to agree. Henry peered astern at the shrimper, the dredge, and the line of our wake.

"Well," Henry said, heading below, "he damn near put the breakfast upside-down on the deck. Pancakes are ready, guys."

"You boys eat first, then one of you come up to relieve me," ordered Dean.

"Shit, that was close," Jack whispered once we were below in the passageway.

"He never slowed down at all," I said.

"Yeah, not one knot," agreed Jack. "He almost grounded us right at the beginning, and did you notice how he neatly squelched anything we could say. That's how he's gotten out of scrapes before this one."

Compared to the leaden pancakes served on most commercial salmon boats in Alaska, the *Scottie*'s were light as a feather. While Henry explained that he made his own batter from scratch, Jack and I demolished a huge stack along with sunny-side-up eggs, glasses of orange juice, and several cups of coffee. Henry was a good cook.

Jack went up and took the wheel. Dean wolfed down his breakfast like a man who had not eaten in a week. When finished, he pushed the plates aside, lit a cigarette and with a pencil and paper worked out the wheel watches based on three hours on and nine off. I was assigned the 1:00 to 4:00 watch. Innocuous in the afternoon, with fatigue this watch became deadly in the black hours of the early morning. I had learned this in Alaska where, by Fate it seemed, I had stood the same watch. With her radar, LORAN, auto pilot, and radio direction finder, *Scottie* promised to be far easier to keep on course at night than the blind Alaskan seiners. The captain stood the watch before mine, and Jack's followed.

CHAPTER IX

THE STORM

Ah! The good old time—the good old time. Youth and the sea. Glamour and the sea! The good, strong sea, the salt, bitter sea, that could whisper to you and roar at you and knock your breath out of you.

—Joseph Conrad, *Youth*

LOGBOOK, DAY 2: JANUARY 4, 1970

By the time I took my first night watch at 01:00 hours, the weather had deteriorated. The short chop of Mobile Bay had given way to abrupt, muscular seas driven before a nasty northeast wind in a black night. Some waves broke over *Scottie*'s port stern quarter.

The captain gave me the compass heading, then went below. I followed a simple checklist learned in the salmon fishery when coming on watch. I peered into the black night, noted the engine temperature and oil pressure, then checked the compass heading, and ended by studying the chart. The *Scottie* steered herself. I settled into the comfortable, high captain's chair, pleased at the glow of red instrument lights of this sophisticated bridge and a little proud to be entrusted with this vessel finally at sea. In the middle of the watch, a big ship passed, headed into Mobile Bay. On this stormy night her lights were too far off to be seen, but she appeared as a solid blip tracking across the whirling green sweep of the radar. I wondered if someone on her bridge had seen the small blip that was the *Scottie*. At 04:00 hours I woke Jack and returned to the bridge. He came up awake and excited. I instructed him on my checklist. We discussed our estimated position, the progress we had made since departure, and the joy of being at sea. Then I headed for my bunk.

The combination of spray blasting through my port hole and a violent roll of the boat awakened me. The bunk was soaked, leaving no choice but to close and dog the port's glass. Without the breeze through the port, the temperature increased quickly. Even with the sheet thrown back, a thin sweat squeezed from every pore.

The boat rolled violently off another big sea. The weather had worsened since my watch. The roll was so steep that it threw me against the bunk boards. I jumped down from my upper bunk and found the light switch. Jack had already returned from his watch and lay on his back, wide awake.

"Where're you going?" asked Jack

"Spray though my port hole woke me up. I'm going for a towel to try to dry it a bit."

"Yeah, I had to shut mine too," said Jack. "Sure made it hot in here."

"Sure did! The deck is hot on the feet."

Just then the boat took a deep roll to port. I grabbed the upper bunk board to keep from falling. Jack had to brace himself in his bunk to avoid being pitched out.

"Hmm," I mumbled, "Heat from the engine warming the decks will be great in Alaska, but not much fun here."

"Wonderful," sighed Jack. "The seas are much bigger than when I took over the watch from you."

I peered out my porthole window from where I stood. For an instant, in the early light of day, I could see breaking seas stretching to a gray horizon. The boat rolled heavily to port, only confirming the worsening conditions.

Quite suddenly, I felt nauseated. The back deck and fresh air had an urgent appeal. The wind strong-armed the watertight door to the aft deck, holding it firmly closed. I had to put a shoulder to it to force it open. The wind screamed in the rigging. I huddled under the overhang of the upper deck at the aft of the deck house near the mast for protection. I took a hand-hold on one of its cleats. The fierce short steep seas broke continuously, hurling their crests over the railing and across the deck. This foul weather was incongruously warm, unlike cold Alaskan storms. Dark clouds scudded low across the horizon. The boat rolled then lurched upright in a continuous, exhausting motion. Nevertheless, the fresh air felt good after the humid heat of the cabin.

As soon as I stepped back inside and secured the watertight door, suffocating heat welled up from the engine room. I darted across the grating in the passage above the engine room, closing the galley door quickly behind me.

Henry attempted to serve lunch, but the plates and food slid violently across the table. Dampened dish towels helped, but taller containers like the ketchup bottle clattered to the deck. Jack and I cleaned up after the meal, which became a permanent assignment. With one hand for the dishes, the other for the boat, cleaning up was an arduous, time-consuming task.

Lunch was difficult; dinner impossible. The wind increased throughout the afternoon. The steep seas built in height, causing *Scottie* to pitch and roll violently. By evening, using all the fiddles on the stove top, Henry could keep only one pot in place. Walking was a series of sprints to the next handhold. The humidity and heat inside the boat increased with every mile sailed south. *Scottie* was often engulfed in hails of spray, forcing closure of all port holes. Only the bridge was above the flying spray. There the side windows were kept open, allowing air movement and creating the coolest place inside the boat.

One particularly severe roll to port half emptied the lone pot of its boiling water. Henry turned to us in exasperation. "That's it," he announced. "I can't keep anything on this damn stove. All it's doing is adding to the heat. It's going to be sandwiches or whatever else you fix for yourselves."

Henry's proclamation came as no surprise, although a forlorn look shadowed Jack's face. I found the prospect of reduced heat from shutting down the galley stove a promising trade-off. The sticky heat so far had stripped us all to shorts and t-shirts. Whether the loss of regular meals influenced the captain could not be determined, but he did order Henry to tank down one of the two live tanks. Filling this tank with seawater, a dangerous operation until the tank was full, lowered *Scottie's* center of gravity. She would be less cork-like in the maddening seas.

By 22:00 hours, I was in my bunk. *Scottie* was rolling so violently that the motion threatened to pitch a relaxed body over the bunk board onto the deck. I wedged myself into my bunk to prevent being catapulted out of it. This wedging demanded contracted muscles. As soon as I fell asleep my muscles relaxed and I awoke, frantically grabbing the side of the bunk to prevent flying out of it. Sleep was impossible.

Jack tried to rig a small fan, purchased at Sears, to keep air circulating in the hot cabin. Despite Jack's efforts to secure it, the fan crashed to the deck twice. When set up on the deck, it emulated a hockey puck caroming off the boards after a slap shot. Jack cradled the fan in the crook of an arm as he lay in the bunk which provided air movement but made falling asleep even more dangerous. While we lay in drowsy agony, there came a bulkhead jarring thud.

"What was that?' said Jack, startled to full consciousness by the unusual sound.

"Don't know," I said quickly.

"Thud,"—the sound was loud but intermittent. It came from the galley. I jumped down from the bunk and fought in the bucking blackness to find the light switch. When I finally located it, sweat was running freely down my face, not all from the heat. I wedged myself in a corner to pull on my boots. Then I bolted out with Jack right behind me. The bare light in the passageway revealed nothing amiss. Henry's cabin door was closed. I headed for the galley and flipped on the light with Jack peering over my shoulder.

All appeared normal. I stepped into the galley but held onto a counter. To my immediate left stood the refrigerator-freezer. *Scottie* took a deep roll. Both upper and lower doors of the refrigerator flew wide open, slamming against the adjacent bulkhead with a resounding thud.

The boat hung in the deep roll for an agonizingly long instant. Suddenly, the entire contents of both the refrigerator and freezer slid out and remained suspended in mid-air just as if still arranged on the shelves. Three weeks' food supply hung there for a mesmerizing second, then dropped with a shattering crash onto the galley floor.

The monumental heap at our feet began undulating with the motion of the boat, spreading out on the hot, pitching deck. The boat jerked back toward level. The reefer doors slammed shut, the lower door crushing a carton of twelve dozen eggs left dangling from a shelf. The door's force nearly cut the carton in half. The carton slithered to the floor bleeding a trail of yellow yolk.

"What the hell was that?" said a voice from behind us. It was Henry. Jack just stepped back to give Henry a full view. He gasped at the mess. He stepped into the galley, letting go of the door jamb at the same instant that his foot landed in the hemorrhage from the egg cartoon and the boat rolled again to port. On that one foot, he suddenly accelerated, arms windmilling wildly. He slid all the way across the galley to the table, which he grabbed, regaining his balance. The reefer doors slammed open again against the bulkhead.

Henry carefully turned to face us. He looked down at the mess on the floor and then at the open refrigerator doors.

"Ah, shit," he said. The boat rolled to starboard, and the doors slammed shut.

The galley floor quickly turned into a swamp. The basic fluid was a thick yoke-colored slime that undulated with each roll of the boat. Cucumbers galloped across the morass followed by slower heads of iceberg lettuce. Green bell peppers wandered about. The tomatoes lay bleeding seedy orange. All the eggs were broken, their shells strewn like the aftermath of a reptilian emergence. To one side, near the overturned dome of a plastic bowl, the tuna fish spread eroded slowly into the ooze. Here and there split milk cartons leaked, steadily expanding the mire.

"What the hell is banging down there?" came a cry from the bridge.

"We're getting it under control," shouted Henry. He slogged back through the swamp to the refrigerator/freezer, keeping a hand on the drainboard all the way. He tried to re-latch the reefer doors. Knowing that the standard magnets could not keep the doors closed in rough seas, the yard had attempted to make the land-based unit seaworthy by adding ten-cent screen door latches. The small hooks proved too weak to secure the doors in these heavy seas. As soon as Henry latched them, with the next wave, the doors slammed open again. Henry wired the doors shut with bailing wire fetched from the engine room. This solution worked but made the simple act of opening a refrigerator door painstakingly difficult in the relentlessly rolling vessel.

"OK," said Henry. "That should keep this two-bit reefer under control for a while. You guys start cleaning up. I'll tell Dean what happened. Save what you can. We've got the food in the deck freezer, but this was our fresh supplies," he said as he stepped into the passage on his way to the bridge.

Jack and I began by wading through the mess to rescue undamaged items. The lubricating film on the deck, consisting of egg, milk, mayonnaise (two big jars had shattered upon impact), butter, thousand island dressing, and orange juice, had the frictional resistance of ice. Having gathered up the few unbroken and undamaged items, we washed them off in the sink. Even the cold-water tap produced hot water.

Jack struggled to hold the refrigerator door open after we had laboriously unwired it. His feet kept sliding in the goo. At times he held the door open and at others it held him up. Meanwhile, I wedged the salvaged food between shelves to keep it from bashing about inside the empty refrigerator. Timing was everything.

"Now," I said. He slammed the door shut and held it while I wired it. I wondered how one person would accomplish this four-handed task to get food out.

Attacking the swamp with a mop had little effect. So much heat radiated up through the deck from the main engine that the eggs had begun to cook. We got down on hands and knees to attack the mess with rags and the remaining paper towels, but soon found that a spatula worked better.

"Jack," I said, looking about at the slowly cooking egg, tomatoes, bell peppers, all mixed in the milk, "this is the world's largest omelet."

"You're right," said Jack. Sweat dribbled down his pasty white face. "I need some air."

Whether it was the power of suggestion or the sour stench emanating from the hot, gyrating galley floor, the debilitating nausea of sea sickness returned. I hurriedly followed Jack out the watertight door, but little relief awaited us on the aft deck. The wind screamed, tearing at our t-shirts. Thundering waves relentlessly materialized at the railing, each intent on shoving *Scottie* over. Sheets of stinging spray burst out of the darkness. Going to the aft deck was a foray into a hellish no-man's land. Quickly we scurried back inside. The aft deck terror of raging wind and stinging spray, plus the very act of being vertical, forced the nausea into a tentative remission. In the hot, messy galley, the nausea persistently recurred.

Periodically we returned to the aft deck, clinging near the door, gulping the fast-moving air, and shielding ourselves from the blasts of spray. We spent hours this way, intermittently mopping and peeling up the mess from the galley floor, then bolting to stand outside in the storm's tumult. We managed to finish about 01:00 hours. Henry returned at the very end, in time only to help us wring out the mop and rags. Before reporting for the wheel watch, I washed the sweat and salt spray from my face and arms. The hot water from the cold tap did not refresh.

"They did a damn stupid thing putting a refrigerator like that on a king crabber," said the captain as I took over the bridge. "Looks like they cut corners everywhere they could." He checked the chart, gave me the course, then went below.

I looked out into the blackness, then peered into the radar screen and stood momentarily entranced in its luminescent, green, sweeping world. I made my way to the chart table, having to grip it firmly, as the motion on the bridge, the highest point of the ship, was more violent than below. Our track made a line reaching south into the Gulf of Mexico from Mobile. After checking the engine gauges, I made my way across the rolling deck to the captain's chair. Bolted to the deck near the starboard windows, it was not going anywhere. As I climbed into it, I suddenly realized how tired I was. Just balancing to stay upright, fighting the incessant wild motions of the vessel, drained endurance. Cleaning up the monumental mess in the galley added to the exhaustion. I hoped to stay awake.

The boat lurched its way across the broken, invisible sea, plunging off the back of a wave, slamming into its trough only to be hurled skyward for another round. Two days out of Mobile seemed an eternity. Any fantasies I had concocted about this voyage were boiling away in the black cauldron of the storm.

CHAPTER X
AT SEA

There was for us no sky, there were for us no stars, no sun, no universe—
nothing but angry clouds and an infuriated sea.

—Joseph Conrad, *Youth*

LOGBOOK, DAY 3: JANUARY 5, 1970

Just before 04:00 hours, Jack emerged on the bridge from the dark stairwell. His hair was sticking out rigidly in wild clumps, stiffened by salt from the sea spray that had peppered us on the aft deck the night before. Demon red rimmed his eyes. Dark puffy half-moons lay beneath each bleary eye.

"How's it going?" he squinted at the impenetrable darkness beyond the bridge's windows.

"Well, we're slugging through it, one wave at a time."

"Hell, I know. It's impossible to sleep in that hot house of a cabin, even if you didn't have to hang on just to stay in the damn bunk."

"You do look a little rough around the edges." I gave him the course. "Probably not enough time in the lounge chair on the aft deck."

"Right," said Jack, with a raised eyebrow.

Whatever joviality I mustered on the bridge was snuffed out when I tried to sleep. The cabin was like a Dutch oven. The boat dropped so precipitously off waves that the half-dozing sleeper was left suspended in air, flailing to regain a handhold. I tried the fan, but the cord would not reach the top bunk. A film of sweat permanently coated my skin. I cracked my port open a fraction for air circulation, but water sprayed in as from a fire hose. The bunk was soaked before I could re-dog the port.

The *Scottie's* aft deck during the storm. Photo by Jack.

When Jack returned from his watch, we ventured to the galley for breakfast. My stomach, partly from nausea and partly from constantly fighting for balance, was knotted. It accepted begrudgingly a piece of bread with a thin spread of peanut butter, washed down by a few swallows of juice.

The rest of the day dragged on and on in the relentless wind and waves. The seas pounding the vessel, the drone of the engine, the lack of sleep all combined to produce a catatonic state in which hours wove into a seamless shroud of dull fatigue. The gray of the day and another wheel watch morphed through a short tropical dusk into impenetrable night.

LOGBOOK, DAY 4: JANUARY 6, 1970

At 01:00, I climbed to the bridge for wheel watch. Dean sat head back, mouth open, asleep in the captain's chair. I cleared my throat loudly a few inches from his ear. He grumbled awake. He quickly, mechanically checked the course, gave it to me and stumbled down the ladder, intent on his bunk. His cabin door slammed shut.

The engine readings were normal. I peered into the radar hood. The height of the breaking waves now showed like snow on the radar screen, dotting the area just beyond the center of its sweeping arm. The windows forward revealed only blackness. An awareness grew, an odd sensation, as if the boat's motion had slowed. She rolled to port and starboard more drunkenly. Yet maybe this perception was a distortion caused by fatigue. I climbed into the captain's chair, but the perception persisted. The boat wallowed precariously in the extreme limit of each roll.

The light switches that activated the aft deck mercury vapor lights were mounted on the rear wall of the bridge, next to the port side rear facing door. King crabbers worked in the long Alaskan night and needed powerful illumination of the aft deck. I flipped the lights on. They took time to kindle to full brightness, but as they did so, pushing back the black night, they revealed green water, not just waves, washing over the deck. Normally, after each sea, the deck rose shedding tons of water. I waited and waited. Only the tops of the railings rose reluctantly out of the green, swirling sea. A black object sloshed in the confines of the railing tops. For an instant, I thought it a body, but saw that one of the three fifty-five-gallon drums of lube oil lashed to the rail had broken loose.

I stood frozen for a long moment while a realization formed out of all the images: the boat was slowly sinking. I suddenly imagined *Scottie* sliding beneath the waves leaving only a 55-gallon drum of lube oil as evidence. Shaking off this illusion, I dove down the bridge steps and hammered on the captain's door.

"Get up, get up, Dean!" I shouted. At last, dull grumbling became audible. The door flung open, revealing the captain in his boxer shorts and black loafers.

"The boat is sinking. Come to the bridge now," I said and turned, bolting up the steps. "There," I said pointing to the submerged aft deck. He stepped to the rear windows, peering at the brightly lit scene. His eyes slowly widened.

"Get Henry up. Tell him to start the pumps!" he yelled.

I leapt down the steps again with the terrible vision of the boat rolling over and sinking.

"Henry," I said, banging on his cabin door, "Get up and start the pumps." Henry was at the door in an instant.

"What?"

"The back deck is awash. Captain says to get the pumps going fast," I said as calmly and clearly as I could.

"Right," said Henry, "but which pumps?"

Stunned, I let him pass. I remembered him, during the sea trials, standing before the wall of valves with a blank look on his face.

He crossed the galley, heading for the passage above the engine room. I followed. He had managed to pull on his tennis shoes and Bermuda shorts. He paused at the top of the engine room ladder, turned and opened the watertight door to the aft deck. The brilliantly lit scene revealed the clear waters of the Caribbean lapping at the high sill of the door.

"Jesus, both tanks must be full!" He slammed the door, latched a couple of its handles, then scurried down the ladder into the engine room. I followed him.

Henry stood in front of the mass of valves. He checked the position of a few. He closed two and opened a couple more mumbling, "Man, what a jumble." If he could not figure out this wall of valves, no one else on board had a clue.

Henry flipped on some switches and pumps began to hum. "Think I got it now," he yelled over the roar of the main. "That should empty the aft tank." He lifted a deck plate. "The bilge is dry," he confirmed.

The heat rolling off the main in the narrow space increased my sense of claustrophobia. I did not want to be down here if the boat sank.

"I'll tell Dean what you found and that you're pumping out the second tank," I said. Henry nodded in agreement, the sweat rolling off his face.

I stopped at our cabin, shaking Jack awake. Somehow he had wedged himself in his bunk securely enough to doze off. Just as he sat up, the barrel of oil slammed loudly into something steel on the deck.

"What's that, what's happening?" Jack shouted. He was completely disoriented.

"The boat is half sunk. One lube oil drum is loose, floating around the deck. That's how low we are in the water. Follow me to the bridge." He jumped from his bunk and pulled on his boots.

"Is Henry pumping her? Is he pumping her?" Dean shouted as we climbed the bridge ladder.

"Yes," I affirmed.

"Take the helm," he said to me as he shot down the stairway.

"Wow!" said Jack, looking at the scene on the aft deck under the bright lights. "Looks like a swimming pool." The oil drum banged up against the main hatch. The deck appeared slightly raised from the surrounding sea compared to the first time the lights illuminated it. The breaking waves still washed across it.

"Jack, when I took over, Dean was asleep in the chair. After he went below, I thought something was strange, but I didn't know what until I got the deck lights on."

"Oh, that's great," said Jack, "and we could have sunk with him asleep at the helm?"

"I don't know, but something sure went wrong to sink us so low in the water." The drum hit a rail with a resounding crash.

Dean returned, charging up the stairway, puffing and sweating.

"Both damn live tanks are full," he gasped. "A seacock must have been left open between the tanks so the one filled from the other. Those idiots at the yard—." At that instant, the barrel crashed again. "Go get Henry, you two, and secure that damn drum. I'll take over."

Down to the engine room we went. "Captain says you need to help us secure that oil drum on deck," I yelled in Henry's ear above the thunder of the main. He gave a thumbs-up sign. Jack did not like the engine room any more than I did and was first to the ladder. He flipped open the latches that dogged the deck door, then leaned on it hard to push it open against the wind. We surveyed the scene from the safety of the doorway. A breaking wave crashed on board. The pumps were working. *Scottie* rose enough out of the sea to send tons of water gushing out the scuppers. The oil drum was swept along in the cascading water until it crashed against a railing. As the boat heeled in the opposite direction, the drum rolled in the turbulence and came to rest against the aft side of the main hatch. Seeing the drum immobile, Henry darted out the door.

"Come on," he shouted, "let's trap it against the hatch." Jack and I leapt after him. The engineer moved surprisingly quickly on his short legs. Our charge had started when the deck was clear of the last sea, but before we reached the aft side of the hatch, another huge sea poured over the rail, sending a knee-high wall of water across the deck. We had to stop to take a grip on the main hatch and instinctively leaned into the oncoming wall of water. I was prepared for a blast of cold sea. The warm water surprised me. Jack groaned loudly as the sea filled his new boots.

With the force of the wave diminishing, Henry sloshed forward to the drum and leaned on it to pin it against the hatch combing. I followed, but before I reached him, he rotated the drum, starting in the direction of the port rail where the other drums were still lashed. He turned his head and yelled something, but I could not hear him above the shrieking wind. I moved to help him, but he began to back up towards me. I almost ran into him. He let go of the drum and turned, a look of terror on his face. The direction of the current had changed and now the half-submerged 400-pound steel drum rolled toward us. Henry and I slogged through the knee-deep water. Jack, greatly slowed by the weight of water in his boots, saw us coming and turned to escape. The three of us ran around the hatch while the bull-like drum swept by, plowing into a railing.

"OK, let's go," yelled Henry.

We charged from behind the hatch, splashing through the receding sea toward the drum. Unfortunately, we arrived just as another big wave hit, sending a thigh-high wall of water at us. I was able to get a good grip on one end of the drum, but Henry and Jack veered away, grabbing the railing to brace against the oncoming sea. With the water's force, the drum twisted out of my grasp. It took off, sweeping toward them on the flood. They broke and ran, splashing away with the rampaging drum threatening to crush their ankles.

Tons of water gushed out of the scuppers. The drum slowed, grounding on deck. I ran up and pinned the drum to the deck, yelling at Jack and Henry for help. They looked over their shoulders in disbelief, but reversed direction, splashing to my aid. The three of us held the beast down before the next sea bore down upon us. The wall of water hit us above the knees. The drum rose from the foaming sea, twisting and pulling. Somehow, this time, like men holding down a wild steer for branding, we controlled the thing enough to shuffle it towards the rail. We pinned it there. The wave drained away. Another sea came crashing aboard but this time, with our combined weight, we managed to keep the drum pinned, quelling another rampage.

"Now what?" Jack grunted through clenched teeth.

"Let's just lash it here," I said.

"With what?" said Henry, panting heavily.

The only other line on deck held the other drums. All other lines were sloshing around in the forward live tank. We could not pull open the hatch covers in the storm.

"Dump this thing overboard before it breaks our legs," yelled Henry.

I wanted to protest, but another wave exploded out of the night, tore along the deck and engulfed us. The drum surged under our combined weight, threatening to break away. The boat rolled hard to port, nearly leveling us with the surrounding sea. In waist-deep water, only the cap of the rail was between us and the black ocean.

"OK, up and over," yelled Henry, seizing the instant.

We crouched, pushed, and rolled the drum upward the last inches to the rail top. *Scottie* rolled back to starboard. The drum balanced for an instant on the top of the rail, then tumbled away into the sea and instantly swept astern, swallowed by the black night. Stunned, the three of us held the rail. Although we had removed the danger from the deck, the chilling disappearance of the drum showed how quickly one of us would vanish if swept over the side. We made our way carefully across the deck to the other drums, re-tightening their lashings. At times we were again waist deep in the sea, but always with one hand gripping the rail.

By the time we scrambled back into the deck house, *Scottie* had raised herself out of the sea. Henry went below to check the pumps. Jack tugged off his new boots, dumping sea water from each. We dug out towels and stood dripping, trying to dry the sticky salt water off in the thick humid air.

"OK," said Henry, returning to the galley. He was still dripping wet. "We've got the second live tank emptying fast."

"Hey," yelled the captain, "What's going on anyway!"

"I'll go talk to him," said Henry squishing away in tennis shoes that left little pools of water tracking along the deck. Jack slumped onto the bench behind the galley table. "Wow, did you see how fast the drum disappeared?" he asked.

"I did," I said trying to pull the drenched T shirt over my head. "We've got to be careful. Anyone over the side is a goner."

"I didn't realize how far down we were in the water until we rolled the drum over. Hell, we were damn near submerged!" said Jack.

Henry popped back into the galley. "Looks like the auto pilot is out. Dean has to steer by hand to hold a course. I couldn't find anything wrong on the bridge but we'll have to check the sending unit in the morning. It's in the lazarette." He was quiet for a moment, then sat down behind the table next to Jack and me. "Hope you guys are good at steering a compass course."

We sat for a long time, dripping small briny pools of water, saying nothing. Our bodies slightly leaned and tipped with the motion of the boat. The ceaseless pounding of the seas, the sleep-robbing heat, the adrenalin-charged chase on the aft deck combined to exhaust us. I looked at the time, 03:00 and realized it was still my watch.

"Guess I better get back to the bridge," I said. We rose slowly. Henry, still squishing in his tennis shoes, padded toward the engine room. Jack preceded me into the passage but turned toward the head.

"Guess I'll leave this wet stuff in here," he mumbled. "Don't want to get the bunk any wetter. Wonder when the sunny part starts?"

"I'm not sure of the sun anymore. I just want to make it to the Panama in one piece," I said.

Peering into the binnacle with its dim white light, Dean was standing at the wheel.

"The damned idiots at the yard," he began. "They sure didn't work out the bugs. That second tank should never have filled. Then the damn auto-pilot goes out. She steers like a tank by hand."

While he talked, he was continuously moving the spoked, mahogany wheel back and forth. He never alluded to his nap at the wheel.

"Here, get the hang of it," he said, offering me the helm, then turning to brood over the chart table.

Scottie, rolling and pitching, responded slowly to multiple turns of the wheel. The tortured sea told its tale in the wild angles of the compass card. The seas striking the stern quarter continuously pushed the vessel off course. Holding the course proved a tiring task. Only the suspended compass card gave a stable point of reference. After a few mumbled curses over the chart, Dean gave me the compass course then went below. The best I could manage—and I had experience on the helm in Alaska—was to bracket the course fifteen degrees on either side. The constant focus to hold the course in the maddening seas with no outside reference made the forty remaining minutes of my watch pass like hours.

When it was time for Jack's watch, I ran down to awaken him. The short time I was away, the boat wandered like a drunkard. Jack arrived fifteen long minutes later. I gave him the course and the wheel, then watched as he struggled with the bucking boat.

"This is murder," he said after five minutes.

"You better believe it," I agreed. "Maybe it will be better in daylight; at least then we'll have the horizon."

"Let's hope Henry can fix the damn auto-pilot," said Jack. "By the way," he added as I started down the steps, "it's still hot as hell in the cabin." And it was.

Sleep came in fits of half consciousness in the struggle to stay in the bunk. When sleep relaxed the muscles too much, the whole body took flight and full consciousness returned in a wild flailing for a grip, and a punishing landing. Some hours into this somnolent torture, the engine suddenly slowed for the first time in two and a half days. Jack was back.

"What's up?" I asked.

"Dean and Henry are working on the auto-pilot." Before Jack could say more, Dean's head popped in through our cabin door.

"Both of you to the bridge," he ordered, then disappeared.

I swung my legs over the edge of the bunk, feeling drugged and tarred with gritty sea salt. Daylight had returned.

"OK," Dean shouted as we appeared on the bridge. "Take the wheel," he said, unfortunately nodding towards me.

"See Henry on the aft deck. He's at the hatch over the lazarette. The auto-pilot sending unit is in there at the rudder quadrant. We're going to pull the hatch so Henry can check it out. You hold her just like this, running before the sea. We don't want any waves on deck." Then he dived down the bridge steps and was gone.

Had I been fully awake when I climbed to the bridge, I would have asked why Dean had not put her bow into the seas. Running before the waves, a big sea could break over the stern pouring through the open lazarette hatch.

At one-third throttle, the boat was even less responsive, demanding more turns of the helm to hold the stern directly before the on-rushing waves.

Jack watched closely as Dean and Henry removed the steel deck hatch, using its special wrench for the task. Dean cut a strange figure, partly because of the soaked boxer shorts, which stuck to his buttocks, but also because he still wore his black dress loafers, which slipped on the wet deck. With the hatch removed, the two of them crouched over the open manhole. Then Henry went forward into the deck house and was gone for several minutes while Dean continued to peer down the hole. Finally, Henry returned.

After a few minutes, Henry climbed into the manhole, slowly lowering himself down in stepped increments. All this time, I had been successful at keeping the waves from breaking on the deck, but then a big one rose up steeply and dumped part of its tumbling crest over the stern rail. The water spread out, threatening the manhole. Dean saw the approaching water, jumped up and waved his hands first right and then left, all the while mouthing words that fortunately I could not comprehend. The water never reached the manhole. The vessel rolled to port, spilling the wave top out the scuppers. With the threat gone, Dean took up his position again at the rim of the manhole. I redoubled my effort to keep the vessel running squarely before the following sea.

After a few more minutes, Dean jumped up and began yelling and waving his arms. No sea had come aboard. We could not make out the message. Jack scurried below to find out what he wanted. After a conference on the aft deck, Jack ran forward and then reappeared on the deck with towels which he handed down the manhole. Dean now took up a position sprawled on the deck, hanging onto the edge of the hole. Jack knelt at the open lip and peered in. Long moments passed in which I struggled at the helm before each wave's foaming crest.

Dean jumped up, slipping across the gyrating deck in his loafers, but making it to the deck house. A moment later he arrived on the bridge, breathless and dripping.

"The damn yard never tightened the lazarette hatch. It was just sitting in the manhole. Water has been pouring in, flooding the whole compartment. We are really lucky we did not sink with two full tanks and a full lazarette. We're pumping it out, but the water level rose so high it submerged the auto pilot. Henry's trying to dry it out. You go back. I'll take a hitch at the wheel."

I made my way across the tilting deck. The wind tore at my t-shirt. I got down on hands and knees next to Jack, getting a secure grip on the lip, and then peered in. A moment passed before my eyes adjusted to the darkness. Henry was standing near the foot of the steel ladder almost directly underneath the opening. About two feet of water crashed back and forth at the bottom of the lazarette, sounding like a gigantic washing machine. Henry stood in the sloshing water, working in a small metal box, from which he had removed the cover. Behind him was the rudder quadrant. It moved menacingly, first in one direction and then the opposite, pushed by big hydraulic rams. Hydraulic hoses jumped under the changing pressure. The mechanical movement of the rams was powerful and indifferent to the fragile human standing nearby.

Henry was firmly planted before the box. The flashlight in his mouth shone on the box's wiry innards. He worked carefully, removing the electrical parts he could, component by component, drying each and delicately replacing it. The minutes ticked by. My knees began to ache on the hard steel deck. Finally, Henry looked up.

"OK, it's as dry as I can get it. Tell Dean to try the auto pilot now."

Jack jumped up and set off for the bridge. Five minutes later he was back, bending over next to me.

"Dean says it's working," yelled Jack into the manhole.

"I didn't fix anything," Henry shouted up. "Hell, we don't have any of these parts aboard, but maybe I got it dry enough to stop some component from shorting."

"Boy, am I glad," Jack said to me. "Steering this beast by hand is a killer, especially at night." As Jack spoke, Henry began carefully replacing the box-like cover. Without warning, *Scottie*'s engine roared. Immediately, the boat surged ahead. She heeled to port, responding to a hard starboard helm turning her to windward.

Within seconds the vessel was broadside to the waves. A huge one broke over the starboard rail sending a wall of water churning toward us. Jack jumped for the port railing, which was the nearest firm hand hold, but, still kneeling, I did not have time to move. I hunched down and held onto the lip of the manhole with all my strength. The wave hit with smashing force that instantly submerged me, but my adrenalin-enhanced grip on the manhole lip and my compact position kept me from being swept away. Before my head went under, I took a deep breath. I remained submerged long enough to wonder what to do if I ran out of breath. Before I had to decide, my head cleared the surface.

Blinking away stinging salt water, I saw tons of water pouring down the manhole as if it were a massive tub drain. I glanced up. Jack had made it to the rail but appeared to be jumping up and down in the swirling current. I got a forearm up and wiped it across my face, which cleared my vision. Jack was indeed jumping up and down. Somewhere, the manhole cover had swept along the deck in the rushing water. Jack, unable to see it, jumped madly to save his ankles.

As suddenly as it had come aboard, the wave roared out through the scuppers. I peered down into the manhole. Henry emerged from the dissipating waterfall. He held to the steel ladder with both hands. Sea water gushed from his pockets and from the just-dried auto pilot box. The water level in the lazarette was to his waist. The flashlight cast an eerie glow from the bottom, rolling back and forth in the undulating water. Henry, without releasing his grip on the ladder, wiped his face against the upper part of an arm.

"What the holy, loving hell are you guys trying to do, drown me and the auto pilot at the same time?" he yelled without looking up.

"The captain just gunned her and turned into the waves. That's when we took the green one over the rail."

"Well, shit," he spluttered bending down to grab the flashlight. "He really drowned the electronics this time."

The engine slowed while the boat completed her turn. Another wave attempted to break on board but the vessel, no longer broadside to the seas, shed it. The last of the water drained out the scuppers. Jack managed to locate the steel hatch cover, stepping on it to prevent further leg-threatening excursions.

Dean burst from the galley's watertight door and made his way across the rolling deck as the boat wallowed at idle. When he reached the manhole, he threw himself prone on the deck and peered into the gloom below.

"Did that water get—," he began to ask but the question caught in his throat as his eyes adjusted to the scene below.

"Christ, did it get in!" shouted Henry, "Any more, and I'd be swimming down here. What the hell were you trying to do?"

"Well, I just wanted to get her head round into the sea to avoid taking one over the transom. It was just rotten luck that one big bastard broke over the side."

"This auto pilot is drenched. Get me more dry towels and I'll try again," said Henry, ignoring the captain's excuses.

Jack went for the towels, but first picked up the manhole cover and wedged it behind the mast. Henry worked on the electronics for another 45 minutes, but when Dean tried the auto pilot again, it remained inoperative. Henry gave up, replaced the cover on the box and climbed out, squinting in the daylight. He said nothing, just squished off toward the deck house. Jack and I were left to dog the lazarette hatch cover, which we did with a vengeance to make sure it sealed.

"Had this been tightened properly in the first place, we wouldn't be in this jam," I yelled.

"It's going to be hell steering the rest of the way to Panama," said Jack.

"Question is, can we get parts to fix this thing in Panama?"

"Oh, man," said Jack as the vessel picked up speed and resumed course. "I just hope we get to Panama."

My watch that afternoon became torture. Steering to the compass became an endurance match against the relentless march of powerful waves, each shoving the boat off course. The three-hour watch felt like six. My arms ached from constantly turning the wheel. Back in my bunk, sleep remained maddeningly elusive in the overheated tumult of the airless cabin.

Henry made tuna sandwiches that evening. The bread, rescued from the refrigerator disaster, was beginning to mold. The captain joined Henry and me at the table. His day's bad luck continued as he lost control of the sandwich plate, dumping half its contents onto the galley deck. I cleaned up. For Jack, still at the helm, it would be another peanut butter and jelly.

CHAPTER XI
NIGHT BALLET

Ah! The good old time—the good old time. Youth and the sea. Glamor and the sea! The good, strong sea, the salt, bitter sea, that could whisper to you and roar at you and knock your breath out of you.

—Joseph Conrad, *Youth*

Despite the steamy heat and the film of salty sweat that glued my skin to the crumpled sheet, I lay frozen in my bunk. Outside the porthole, the black Caribbean night pressed down upon the stormy sea. The only sound above the constant thrum-thrum of the diesel main engine was the splashing wake as the boat rolled and pitched through the angry waves.

Doubting the senses that had roused me, I peered into sheer darkness. Suddenly a thunderous *klongg* exploded, emanating from everywhere in the steel vessel as if it had been struck by a huge maul.

"What the hell is that!" came Jack's terrorized whisper from the lower bunk.

"I don't know," I whispered back, "but we better find out." I did not move.

The boat plunged off another wave, rolling hard to starboard. An instant later the shattering metallic crash resounded again. This time the sound, like an electric shock, catapulted me from my bunk. Somehow I landed on my feet, and took two steps forward, groping in the maddening darkness for the light switch.

The boat, having rolled deeply to starboard, began to right herself, careening back to port. I found the switch. Harsh light illuminated our tiny cabin, accentuating the stifling heat.

"Where're you going?" asked Jack, peering bleary eyed from his bunk.

"To find out what's making that noise," I hissed.

I struggled to pull on a boot. The deep port roll threw me against the bunks.

Klonggg—the metallic crash came at the depth of the roll. The reverberating steel ejected Jack from the lower bunk. The boat heaved back toward starboard. I regained my balance long enough to pull on my other boot.

Hauling open the cabin door against a deepening port roll, I stepped into the bare light of the passage. Opposite, the chief engineer's cabin door was closed. Aft, the light from the passage barely penetrated the darkness of the galley. Forward, the light illuminated the closed door of the captain's cabin and the base of the companionway ladder up to the bridge. Nothing appeared amiss.

Klonggg—the terrible smithy was still at work.

"What in hell is going on!" yelled the captain from the top of the bridge's companionway ladder. "Is anyone down there?"

"Yes," I yelled. "We'll find out."

"Hurry up," he shouted.

The next crash seemed to originate somewhere aft. I headed for the darkened galley.

"Shit," said Jack, still struggling to pull on his boots.

Entering the galley, I flipped on the light. In that stainless steel and linoleum realm, all appeared in order. I crossed the galley, passing through the inner door into the short passage to the watertight aft deck door. I flipped on a switch, illuminating the engine room.

The metallic crashing sound had been ominously still for some moments. While I stood staring down the ladder into the engine room, adrenalin-charged scenarios raced through my mind. What if a generator set had broken loose and punched a hole in the hull with the sea pouring in? The boat would soon roll over and slip quickly beneath the dark waves. I waited for the sound to explode from the engine room, but only heat and the chest-vibrating thrum of the diesel rose up from below.

"Open the door," yelled Jack, right into my ear. I jumped a foot in the air.

"Jesus, it's bad enough without you trying to scare me to death!" I yelled back, above the engine noise. I thought I saw a fleeting grin dissolve at the corner of his mouth.

"Well?" he asked, pointing to the watertight door to the aft deck.

The door had a stainless steel knob and six large latching handles to seal it against the sea. Curiously, only one of these was dogged. I grabbed it with one hand and the knob with the other, bracing myself in the doorjamb in preparation for swinging the heavy door open against the boat's violent rolling. I cracked the door open an inch, feeling the roaring wind tug at it. Seeing nothing, I took a deep breath and shoved the door open wider. The open door threw a shaft of light across the deck. The remnants of a wave sloshed toward the scuppers. A figure leapt out of the black night into the light. Not stopping, it bounded toward the port railing and back into the shadows. The thing defied gravity in a grotesque pirouette.

I was siezed by a violent urge to slam the door shut, which was then countered by intense curiosity about the very existence of this flying body. In this riot of conflicting emotion, a small inner voice piped up, "Looks like the engineer!"

Henry was over forty and stout—a combination of age and physique that precluded the soaring leap just witnessed. Even now, from the shadows near the port railing, this ethereal being distinctly yelled, *"Help!"*

Then the world exploded—KLONGGG*!!!*

I ducked and, with adrenalin strength, leapt back into the passage, slamming the heavy steel door behind me. I glimpsed Jack jumping all the way back to the galley door. Before the last reverberations of the sound dissipated, Jack and I were shoving open the watertight door again.

"Helllp!" came the cry from the darkness. The boat began to roll back to starboard. With the predictability of a pendulum, the body swung into the shaft of light, stubby arms extended dance-like above the rotund body. It was Henry. I reached for the switch to the mercury vapor lights. The engineer was swinging across the back deck, but how? Why?

As the kindling mercury vapor drove back the black night, I peered up the mast, which stood a few feet to my left, just aft of the deck house. One of the two booms attached to it, which would haul the 700 pound steel king crab pots, swung freely toward starboard with the deepening roll of the vessel. Somehow it had come unlashed.

"HELLPP!" wailed the soaring engineer again.

Jack and I rushed aft, determined to save the engineer as his trajectory carried him over the raging Caribbean. We caught him midway into his starboard swing as the boom crashed into its stops, emitting another jarring crash. Jack had leapt into the air, grabbing the cargo hook from which Henry swung. I dug my shoulder into the engineer's doughy mid-section. Jack's momentum pancaked his body into Henry's. Our combined impact forced the air from the engineer's lungs in an audible "oof."

Jack's hands landed on top of Henry's, effectively pinning the engineer's fingers around the hook. As soon as he could draw a full breath, the engineer yelled, "LET GO!"

When my feet hit the deck, I dug in, and Jack did the same. Skidding and sliding on the steel deck, we fought the tremendous inertial force of the pendulum engineer. Through combined effort, while ignoring his groans, we substantially reduced his arc of travel. After sliding to port and then to starboard with the roll of the boat, we realized we could not secure the boom by arresting the flight of the engineer.

Henry, longest at this game, and with the clarity that comes with intense pain, began yelling intelligible sentences. "Stop, stop, we can't secure the boom this way," he yelled.

Jack understood immediately. "Go up and secure the damn boom," he yelled.

"Right," agreed Henry through clenched teeth.

Nominated by process of elimination, I released my bear hug on the engineer and ran to the ladder to the upper deck. Climbing through stinging spray, I had no idea what to look for. From the beginning of this delivery voyage, we'd had more pressing problems to worry about than double checking boom lashings. I ran across the upper deck to the mast. The collars with the pin brackets allowing the boom to rotate were welded to the mast at this level.

Checking the base of the errant boom, I immediately saw a huge bolt lying in the lip of the boom collar, below a hole. I grabbed the bolt and jammed it into the hole. As the boom swung, holes aligned, the bolt slipped through and brought the boom to a jarring stop. Wedged on the other side of the boom collar from where I found the bolt was a huge nut. I grabbed it and spun it onto the threads of the bolt. I was amazed that both the nut and bolt had wedged into the collar when they fell out. One or both pieces could easily have been lost to the sea.

"I've got it," I yelled down to Jack and Henry who both still clung to the now docile cargo hook. They stared at the boom, then Henry, ashen-faced, tugged his flattened fingers from beneath Jack's grip. He grimaced as he slowly flexed them, turning his hands as if to make sure that the fingers were still attached.

I descended the ladder and made my way across the pitching deck. Jack still clung tightly to the hook.

"The locking pin fell out. The yard must not have tightened its nut," I said, noticing the wind's force was muting my words. "Why did you grab the hook?" I yelled.

"No choice," Henry yelled back. "When I stepped onto the back deck to investigate the noise, the hook came flying at my head. Barely had time to grab the damn thing before it hit me in the face. That's when the ride began and I didn't dare let go! Let's secure that hook before it gets away again and rips someone's head off."

Henry, in a seaman's low gait, sprinted to the hydraulic winch just aft of the deckhouse. Jack maneuvered the hook to a steel padeye welded at the base of the port rail. He held the hook in the eye while Henry, operating the winch levers, took a hard strain on the cable. He then locked the winch. Without another word, he entered the deck house.

For a moment, Jack looked over the port rail at the white foam wake trailing into the angry black sea. He turned making his way slowly across the deck toward the cabin door.

"Jesus, what next?" he asked as he passed.

CHAPTER XII
THE COAST OF CUBA

LOGBOOK, DAY 5: JANUARY 7, 1970

After getting the engineer and the boom under control, I reported to the bridge for my wheel watch at 01:00 hours. I could not remember when I had last slept.

With the prolonged storm and the loss of the autopilot, the captain had become increasingly worried about navigation. Despite the two LORAN sets, two radar, and the automatic direction finder, Dean doubted each position plotted. He complained about the LORAN sets. He announced he could no longer read the characters on one. Despite the heavy overcast that resembled gloomy twilight, he said too much light reached the screen. To cut the light down, he fashioned a visor from an empty carton of Camel cigarettes and attached it over the screen with duct tape. He twisted the other set's dials frantically and ended each session by slapping its side.

When I arrived on the bridge, Dean gave me the wheel and the compass course. Then he worked at the chart table to fix our current position. He grumbled at the chart, consulted the LORAN with the make-shift visor, then turned to the other LORAN set. He ratcheted the knob, cursed, and smacked the set. He bent over the chart, transferring a line with a set of parallel rules. The low glow of the gooseneck light illuminated sweat that glistened in droplets along his forehead. A slow-burning cigarette dangled precariously from a dry lower lip. After drawing the line, he fumbled angrily for an eraser. Droplets of sweat splashed onto the chart. He erased madly for a few seconds until the paper, weakened by the sweat, tore.

"God damn it!" he shouted, straightening and flinging the eraser. It ricocheted off the chart table, hit a stern-facing window, and disappeared into the surrounding shadows. "The damn chart tore right where I needed to mark our position."

He grabbed a pencil and made a twirling mark right through the hole in the chart. "That's where we are," he announced. "Hold your present course," he yelled, then stumped angrily down the stairs, slamming his cabin door.

Merchant sailing ship captains often locked their charts away after plotting a new fix. It struck me that, in addition to ensuring control, that act forestalled any discussion about navigational accuracy. I began to worry that the captain did not know our position.

I woke Jack at 04:00 hours. I returned to the bridge but waited another 15 minutes before he arrived. Back in the cabin, despite the suffocating heat and the incessant bucking, I dropped into a blank sleep.

"Wake up, wake up," Jack was pushing my entire body. "Come on, wake up."

I opened my grit-filled eyes. Jack's face, close to mine, was blurred. Behind his head, a naked light bulb seared my struggling vision. A glance out the porthole revealed only blackness.

"What's the matter?" I asked. "What time is it?"

"It's still my watch, but Dean's on the bridge. He's a wreck. About half an hour after I took the wheel, I saw something strange on the radar screen, miles away, a shape like a small island. After a few minutes, a couple more appeared on the screen. Nothing like them is shown on the chart, so I woke Dean so he could check them out. He just went nuts. He said it's the coast of Cuba. We've changed course three times since I got him up, but he doesn't trust my steering. He wants you on the bridge."

At first, I absorbed Jack's story into my dream, which also dealt with Dean's erratic behavior, until I realized I was awake, and Jack's tale was a reality.

"Well, if we're going to pile this thing on the coast of Cuba, I'd rather be at the helm than in this bunk," I said, pushing my leaden body upright onto the edge of the bunk.

"Take the wheel," Dean shouted at me as soon as Jack and I arrived on the bridge. Like a caged wild animal, he paced between the radar and the chart table. The red glow of his cigarette pulsed in the darkness.

"God damn, check these islands," he ordered, pulling me off the wheel to the radar screen. Jack grabbed the helm. "Must be the coast of Cuba, but how did we get so far off course? Maybe the compass is way out. Hey, maybe that's it, maybe the compass was improperly adjusted."

Jack told him that we'd witnessed the compass adjuster do his job professionally. Meanwhile, I studied the sweeping world of green on the radar screen. Ahead, distinctive blotches stretched along the horizon. I counted five before Dean hauled me from the scope.

"Here, let me have another look. You check the chart," he ordered, pushing me impatiently toward the chart table.

The last plotted position was still the hole in the chart far from Cuba. Nevertheless, I inspected the nearest reaches of the Cuban coastline but found no landforms even vaguely like the radar blips. I was relieved as the thought of grounding on a forbidden Cuban shore had increased the knot in my stomach. I scanned other lands on the chart. If *Scottie* was far enough off course to be close to Cuba, she could be off in another direction approaching another land mass with a crop of small outer islands, but nothing matched that scenario either.

"Boy, we're closing with them fast. You get back on the wheel," he yelled, hauling me away from the chart table. As soon as I took over from Jack, who seemed all too willing to give up the helm, the captain ordered a new course turning us almost 90 degrees from southerly to westerly. Dean returned to the radar scope. Jack, peering into the void, shook his head.

"Jesus, we've really sailed into them. Come around to 020 now. These islands are all over. Get Henry up. We may be on the beach yet before this is over!"

Dean put the sleep-dazed Henry through the same routine I'd experienced. The captain wanted someone, anyone, to help him out of this navigational nightmare, but would trust no other opinion. Henry, detecting the frenzied mood, looked at the blips on the radar screen but said nothing. Dean hauled him off the screen.

"OK, bring her to 220," he ordered with his face pressed into the radar's hood. I spun the wheel and waited for the boat to turn beneath the compass card. Before the course, I slowed the turn, bringing the rudder amidships. In the dark night, the vessel pounded through unseen but violent seas.

"Is that 220?" asked the captain, taking a long draw on his cigarette during a break from the scope.

"Yes," I answered.

He glued his face back to the radar's conical rubber hood. "Shit, bring her to 180." I did so. Jack and Henry quietly left the bridge.

"Damn," said Dean, "they're all around us." He slowed the engine to one-third speed. "Hey, flip on that depth sounder so we can see when we get into shallow water." The sounder warmed up and could find no bottom. "I suppose that thing is on the blink now, too," was Dean's irritated comment. He again returned to the radar scope. "Bring her to 090," he said.

"090," I answered and turned the boat to the east. And so it went for another half an hour.

"Jesus, we're surrounded. No way out," said Dean grabbing the throttle and slowing the main engine to idle, then pulling the gear lever to neutral. "No choice but to wait for daylight. Shouldn't be long now."

The change in engine speed and uneasy wallowing of the *Scottie* brought Jack and Henry back, wide-eyed, to the bridge.

"OK," announced Dean, "we're holding to daybreak so we can get a fix on these damn islands and shoals. No use putting her on the beach. Go make us some coffee, Henry."

"It's still my watch," said Jack to me. "I'll take over while you catch some sleep." His conscience was getting to him after leaving me with the maniacal skipper. Dean did not protest, so I relinquished the wheel and stumbled down to my bunk.

With the vessel in neutral, I opened my port. No spray, nothing but a blessed breath of air blew through as I lay my head on the crumpled pillow.

I awoke in terror from a leaden sleep, drenched in sweat, bolt upright in the bunk. The vessel was at cruising speed. Spray showered in through the open port hole. The crashing sound of the wake thundered through the port as the boat rose and fell over the mountainous seas. Why wasn't the boat in neutral? I shut the port, looking for land across the daylight sea, but only white caps broke to the horizon. Why was the boat going so damn fast? I lurched out of the cabin for the bridge.

Only Jack was at the helm. He was bent over the binnacle, his back to me as I ascended the stairs.

"What are you doing? What are you doing?" I yelled. He jumped turning quickly to look at me.

"I'm steering this damn boat."

"Jesus, slow her down," I said still fearing the boat near land.

"What?" said Jack.

"Slow her down, Jack. Why are we going so damn fast?"

"We're at cruising speed," said Jack. "You look like hell. Take it easy."

"Where are the islands? Aren't we in the islands?"

"Oh," said Jack. "Come up here and take a look around."

I followed Jack's advice. There was only the sea in every direction except on the port side. There a black squall paraded along the horizon with gossamer tentacles of rain lashing the surface of the sea.

"There's one of your islands," said Jack pointing at the black squall.

"What?"

"Rain squalls," he said. "You spent half the night steering around rain squalls. Look at the radar.

Stunned, I checked the radar. One of the "islands" appeared on the scope where the black cloud hunted along the sea. *Scottie* had spent hours turning one way and another to avoid rain squalls sweeping across miles of open sea. None of the navigational instruments had been wrong. Only the captain's doubt about our position caused the gross misinterpretation of the blips on the radar screen. Fatigue and an unwillingness to challenge the frenzied skipper implicated us all in the long night's farce.

"Holy shit," I whispered.

"Yeah, 'holy shit' is about right," confirmed Jack.

"What did Dean say?"

"Not much, but he blamed it on the LORAN because we've lost contact with the U.S. stations, and none exist along the Mexican coast. So says the Coastal Pilot. He dug out that book after daybreak. Said he suspected the blips on the screen weren't islands all along, but he stopped just to be on the safe side."

"Sure, sure—I wonder if we will make it to Panama?"

"Me too," said Jack. "Henry told me he's never seen Dean this jumpy before, never." He paused to look at me. "As soon as I get off watch, I'm going to get more sleep. You better do the same."

I went below but tried to clean up first. In the head, I flipped on the light. I looked in the mirror. Salt-matted hair stood out all over in clumps. My eyes were red narrow slits with puffy bags underneath. A stubble of a beard peppered my cheeks and chin. My t-shirt was grimy, but the sea was far too rough for a shower. I conjured up a cooling sponge bath, but the water from the sink's cold tap remained almost too hot to touch. I drew water into the sink but most of that sloshed out onto the deck. With perseverance, I got water onto a washcloth and scrubbed most of the salt from my face. Shaving was out of the question. A fresh t-shirt, however, dug arduously from a drawer, added immensely to my sense of cleanliness.

I awakened from partial sleep just before noon. Peering over the edge of my bunk, I saw Jack below me in his bunk, hanging on and awake. *Scottie* was running nearly broadside to the waves. The rolling motion was violent. We struggled into the galley and managed, without breaking the jars, to piece together two peanut butter and jelly sandwiches.

The captain continually interrupted my afternoon watch. *Scottie* was closing with the Yucatan Peninsula. Soon *Scottie* would have to make a major course change to the southeast. Dean hauled up more charts from his cabin, calculated repeatedly, and chain-smoked, but said little. The wind continued to veer but did not diminish. When Dean gave the new course heading, the seas came from the port bow, slightly easing the boat's motion. Now and then sunlight blasted through holes in the overcast. Whitecaps dazzled against vibrant blue water. The wind never decreased. Spray streamed down the bridge windows. The hours of my watch dragged by.

The battle with the sea continued. Inside, the battle translated into a relentless struggle to stay upright, to keep from being thrown into a bulkhead or pitched head long down a stairwell. The merciless, humid heat squeezed from each pore a constant dribble of ineffective sweat, depleting the body fluids. The dehydration and the diet of peanut butter yielded constipation. I entered the head with the promise of my first bowel movement since leaving Mobile.

The toilet was mounted fore and aft. With shorts down and one hand on the bulkhead to my left, I got seated but the boat rolled hard to starboard. The plastic seat, designed in the American heartland where sideways force was unimaginable, sheared off cleanly and sent me sprawling across the deck. Angrily, I struggled too quickly to my feet with my shorts still about my ankles. Hobbled, I could not cope with the steep deck and pitched forward in bare-assed ignominy with the seat clattering about my head. Lying on my back, feet in the air, I tugged my shorts close enough to my waist to stand again without falling. I was lucky to have locked the head door so no one witnessed these naked acrobatics. I caught the toilet seat and jammed it behind the tank. I had no choice but to sit on the rim of the bowl, but my gymnastics cemented the constipation.

"Toilet seat is a goner," I announced to Jack.

"What?" he asked from half sleep.

"Yep, broke right off sideways. Boat's falling apart slowly but surely." I turned out the light and climbed carefully onto the sticky sheets.

CHAPTER XIII
ROGUE WAVE

She tossed, she pitched, she stood on her head, she sat on her tail, she rolled, she groaned, and we had to hold on while on deck and cling to our bunks when below, in a constant effort of body and worry of mind.

—Joseph Conrad, *Youth*

LOGBOOK, DAY 6: JANUARY 8, 1970

My Thursday morning watch became an aching eternity. Chasing the heading on the oscillating compass produced vertigo and subtle sea sickness. Legs and back ached from standing for hours on the steel deck.

Steering became increasingly difficult. More revolutions of the wheel produced only sluggish responses. Finally, the hands of my wristwatch read 04:00. I woke Jack. I felt I could sleep for a week, but back in my bunk, the rolling seas were no place for a nap. As I dozed on the sweaty sheet, my grip on the bunk rails inadvertently relaxed; I then awoke in mid-air, like a dropped cat, twisting to land safely as the boat rocketed upward to meet the next wave crest. Dawn snapped to daylight with the same tropical abruptness as dusk turned to night. The light revealed ranks of mountainous seas marching ceaselessly to the horizon. Despite my fatigue, the heat drove me to the bridge, to stand in the breeze by its open side windows.

Jack stood at the helm. Dean sweated over the chart, looking for Swan Island. The high rocky island offered the first opportunity for a true land sighting in days. Finding it would confirm *Scottie*'s position and the captain's navigation. If we could not find it, we would re-enter the nightmare of being lost on the sea.

Tattered by the howling wind, the scudding clouds tore open with stunning sunlight turning patches of sea deep blue. Foam from dazzling white caps streamed away in straight trails over the lashed surface. Suddenly the light caught the white wings of a tern soaring above the waves. No birds had been sighted for days, so hope rose that we were near land.

"There, there it is, isn't it?" shouted the captain, his face glued to the radar. "Here, have a look," he said to me. I had wedged myself into the gap between the end of the steering console and the sliding window at the port side of the bridge, but I made my way to the radar screen. Dead ahead, at the end of the green rotating arm, was a small solid blip.

"That is land for sure," I said, wanting to be positive.

"Get the binocs and keep your eyes peeled," ordered Dean. "We can't miss it, we just can't. Jesus, hope it's not a ship!" From the corner of my eye, I saw Jack ever so slightly shake his head again.

Soon the binoculars confirmed the radar's finding. The rocky island jutted high out of the sea, spotlighted in a broad patch of sunlight. After a while we could make out great fans of spray exploding up rocky cliffs. White shreds of clouds scudded the island's pinnacle. The sun glinted on the white wings of wheeling sea birds. Dean was elated. Jack and I were elated too. Our days of doubt about our location evaporated.

"Ha, ha," crowed Dean, "Had us right on the mark all along. That's the trouble with a new boat. You just don't know what to trust, but I had it right the whole damn time." Neither Jack nor I could doubt the now triumphant captain, but his bravado masked incompetence.

The seas were mountainous, breaking above bridge level and striking on the port bow. We motored on and on. The sun dazzled and the island receded astern. Dean was at the chart table with Jack at the helm. I stood in my favorite spot by the sliding window at the port side of the bridge. The open window maximized the breeze while its sill provided an excellent hand hold.

The seas appeared steeper, or was it the play of sunlight on translucent crests at the instant before they broke? *Scottie* valiantly climbed over each, then dropped down the backside in a roller coaster plunge. Suddenly there came a sea bigger than the others. Cresting high above us, we rose to it, from a trough much deeper than previous. The following wave was a monster, blanking out the sky. Its crest became concave, like the hood of an immense cobra drawing back to strike. Dean was at the chart table, his back toward the bow. Concentrating on the compass, Jack was at the wheel, head down. The wall of water broke, hurling itself at the bridge.

"Look out!" was all I had time to shout. I ducked, instinctively clinging to the sill. The wall of water slammed *Scottie* hard over onto her starboard side. I saw the captain's feet, still in those dress loafers, slide out from under him. He hung for an instant from the thin mahogany railing of the chart table, then it broke away. In a hail of splintering wood, pencils, and charts, Dean flew across the bridge and neatly clipped Jack's feet out from under him. Then everything disappeared in the seawater exploding through the open window. For an eternal, vividly clear instant, I hung from the sill, seawater pouring over me. The stunned boat lay on her side, indecisive about whether to right herself or yield to the tons of green water and roll over. Suddenly, the water stopped gushing over me. The boat shuddered and struggled back upright. As the water cleared from my face, I saw Jack and Dean in a wet heap of charts and debris against the starboard side of the bridge. Jack lay on top of the skipper, who luckily had landed feet first on the side of the bridge. Jack struggled to get up. He was on top of the hapless captain but scrambled to his hands and knees. The captain was spluttering curses in rage and terror. As soon as he could get on his feet, Jack sprinted back to the wheel.

The next wave was mercifully smaller than the monster that had broken over us. Jack spun the wheel hard to port, bringing the bow directly into the wave. *Scottie* rode up and over it. Now Dean was up, dripping wet, swearing, staring hard out the front windows. The waves as far as the eye could see were large and breaking, but nothing like the giant that had knocked us on beam ends. Pencils clattered about the deck and tumbled down the stairs under Henry's feet as he struggled up the bridge ladder. His face was pale white, his eyes wide.

Dean still held a piece of chart table railing in one hand. "Damn cheap construction," he said, throwing the molding down. "Yeah, we took a green one right over the bridge," he told Henry, who was surveying the mess. "Better go down and check the engine room." Henry turned and descended with a tight-lipped shake of the head. "You guys clean up this mess," Dean ordered as he too left the bridge.

I turned partly to close the sliding window and partly to direct my uncontrollable laughter to the wind so that the departing captain could not hear it.

When I looked back, Jack was bent over the wheel, racked with laughter. The breaking rogue wave had nearly capsized *Scottie,* creating bone-deep fear. Blame it on youth, or on numbing fatigue, but we chose only to see the slapstick scene of Jack thrashing to his feet on the hapless captain rather than the brush with death. The captain, boxer shorts sticking to his white buttocks, black dancing shoes gushing water, was comic relief.

With the paroxysms of laughter ebbing, I went below finding the last two dry towels on board and returned to clean up the bridge. All the electronic gear was wet including the LORAN sets mounted on the ceiling. I dried everything carefully; amazingly, all the devices worked when checked, except one. "Hey," Jack said, as I was finishing, "the binnacle light is out." After gathering up all the soggy charts and the scattered navigation tools, I sought out Henry with that information.

Henry was already on his way to the bridge with glue, hammer, and nails to repair the damaged chart table. The result was strong, but the protruding nails reminded us of Frankenstein's monster. The critical binnacle light proved a more challenging repair. Henry changed the bulb but got no light. He searched but found no short. Without the light, we could not see the compass card at night.

Henry left the bridge and returned shortly with a tin can salvaged from the trash. He had selected one large enough to hold a standard size flashlight and had made a small hole in the bottom, inserting a short copper tube that focused the light into a narrow beam. He screwed the can to a board which he then secured to the polished wood trim above the binnacle with a very large, galvanized nail. This jury-rigged apparatus worked well, keeping the bridge dark except for the necessary illumination of the compass card, but its appearance gave an impression of being nailed to the Cross. Of greater concern was that fact that the steel can and nail might affect the magnetic compass, but there was no way to gauge that in our current circumstances.

Late in the day, the clouds closed ranks, blotting out the sun. The island had long since disappeared below the horizon. The gray seas remained.

CHAPTER XIV
FINDING THE CANAL

The world was nothing but an immensity of great foaming waves rushing at us, under a sky low enough to touch with the hand and dirty like a smoked ceiling.

—Joseph Conrad, *Youth*

LOGBOOK, DAY 7: JANUARY 9, 1970

During my black watch on Friday, the boat steered more irascibly than ever. Each course correction required multiple turns of the wheel. My arms ached with the constant battle to hold course. The drone of the diesel was mind-numbing. Hours of standing on the steel deck created pain that began in my feet, spread upwards into my legs and attacked my lower back. The vessel rose and fell, rolled and pitched, pounded by the incessant parade of unseen waves. Meanwhile my sleep deprivation continued in the overheated, paint-shaker confines of the cabin. I lay awake for a tormented hour, then got up and made my way back to the bridge.

In the inky blackness, Jack was only visible as a denser darkness. I approached quietly, feeling my way. Jack had not heard me; he had his face as close to the compass as possible while leaving room for the wheel spokes to clear his chest. The flashlight batteries were dying, and the beam had dwindled to a meager glow. Jack had adjusted, bending further and further forward to see the fading compass card. In his fatigue, he failed to realize the dimming of the bulb.

"Jack," I said. He jumped. "You're going to be inside that binnacle in a minute."

"Shit, you scared the hell out of me. What are you talking about?"

"Look," I pointed, laughing, "the flashlight is about dead."

"Oh no," he said, "I thought my eyes were going. Get some new batteries."

With the flashlight at full strength, Jack's back found relief in standing nearly vertical. He and I discussed the sluggish steering and the difficulty it added to holding the compass course. Something had changed. We agreed to ask Henry to check the steering. Then I went back to my bunk and, despite the rolling, pitching madness, managed to wedge myself in for nearly two hours of sleep.

After daylight pried its way under the malevolent, gray overcast, Henry checked the steering system under the console on the bridge. No hydraulic leaks, nothing seemed out of order. The steering remained stubbornly slow. Fatigue made all perceptions suspect. Perhaps we only *felt* that the steering was lethargic when it was actually functioning normally.

The storm had not abated. Friday's hours were an endless parade of breaking seas, the reeling boat, elemental food, and torture at the helm to steer the course. In addition, *Scottie* rolled more heavily to port, dipping deeply before hauling herself upright.

The port list bothered the captain. On three occasions, he sent Henry into the engine room to check bilges and pumps. Jack and I were ordered to the aft deck in the howling wind and spray to lift the main hatch and investigate the cavernous live tanks, but we saw no abnormal levels of seawater. Dean came to the unfounded belief that Henry was burning fuel unevenly from the diesel tanks, resulting in the uneven trim. Henry disputed this theory but to no avail. Dean ordered him to rig a hose with a pump to transfer fuel from the port tank to the starboard tank. Henry used a spare pump and ran a hose around the foredeck, which was the shortest distance from the port fuel filler pipe to the starboard one. At mid-day the transfer began.

The captain stationed me at the wheel. *Scottie* had been slowed and turned downwind. With the boat in this orientation, the deck house offered some protection from the wind and following seas. Dean positioned himself at the starboard fill pipe. From the bridge, Jack and I could see the captain as he bent over the pipe. In addition to the ever-present boxer shorts and the black loafers, the skipper had donned a billowy, white, short-sleeved shirt. A pack of cigarettes nestled in the shirt's breast pocket. Henry went below to start the pump.

The captain remained patiently holding the hose in the fill pipe. Suddenly, he recoiled, engulfed in a whale's spout of atomized diesel mist. He held his ground and attempted to jam the hose further down the fill pipe. The problem was not the length of hose down the pipe but the rush of diesel in the tank. Great gusts of air exhausted from the filler pipe, atomizing the incoming fuel and whooshing it skyward. Dean attempted to seal the gap between the walls of the fill pipe and the hose with his hands, but for a third time he was engulfed in a diesel spout. This blast signaled retreat. Dean began yelling, looking up to the bridge and drawing a finger across his throat to stop the pump.

Simultaneously, the deck pitched. The pool of diesel in which Dean stood transformed the steel deck surface into something akin to a hockey rink. *Scottie*'s bow pitched up. As the angle steepened, the captain, still gesticulating and shouting but standing still, shot off down the deck. He latched onto the railing with both hands, managing to arrest his slide but holding on in a near horizontal position. Jack doubled over with laughter as he staggered down the bridge steps to tell Henry to stop the pump.

The diesel ceased spouting from the fill pipe, and Jack returned to the bridge. Henry appeared on the bow. He clung to the rail, struggling to keep his feet beneath him on the slippery deck. Working his way carefully to the fill pipe, he pulled the diesel hose and screwed on the fuel cap. Meanwhile, Dean, drenched in diesel, clung to the rail like a weary prizefighter on the ropes. His once billowing shirt stuck to his skin in big translucent patches. His hair was plastered to his head. The cigarettes, having spilled from his shirt pocket, were scattered about the deck, dissolving into strings of paperless tobacco. When Henry finished securing the fuel cap, Dean said a few words to him that we could not hear. Then the two of them, moving aft carefully on the less treacherous port side, disappeared from our view. The port list persisted.

Henry arrived on the bridge and dispatched Jack and me to clean up the foredeck. We collected mops, a bucket, and Joy dishwashing detergent. (This soap had the power to cut through the diesel.) On our way, we passed Dean on the aft deck attempting to swab the diesel off himself using the last of the paper towels.

The wind screamed and tore at us as we set to work. We had no better time of it on the slippery, pitching deck than Henry or Dean, but we did manage to spread the Joy over the diesel and mopped at it with sea water.

When we signaled to the bridge that we were finished, the boat turned back to the course. The throttle was pushed forward to cruising speed. Once again, sheets of spray blasted the forward half of the vessel. The rest of January the 9th slid by in a haze.

LOGBOOK, DAY 8: JANUARY 10, 1970

Saturday's black watch was yet another numbing three hours. The heat was omnipotent, the storm endless, and the seas infinite. How the engine ran night and day or the radar turned hour after hour were inexplicable. From a voyage that seemed never to start, we now seemed caught in a voyage without end.

Jack was shaking me awake from another half sleep. He was like a raving animal. His hair wild, his eyes red slits, a stubble spattered across his upper lip and around his chin. He spoke quickly. At first, I couldn't make out his words. Then one word sliced through: "LAND."

"LAND!" he shouted, "No doubt about it. We've got it on the radar—a solid line. No rain squalls this time although they are all over the horizon. It's long, it's the coast of Central America!"

For an odd instant, the thought of land was repulsive. This damn thing, land, would break the routine which had become existence. Then I leapt from my bunk and charged to the bridge with Jack on my heels.

The four of us were on the bridge. Despite the mid-day hour, the sky was dark. Black rain squalls patrolled the horizon. I put my face to the rubber eye shield of the radar. To the south on the scope, the sweeping arm scribed a solid line. All else on the screen was transient: dissipating wave tops and ethereal rain squalls. The line was solid land.

"Damn," said Dean, "We had to close with the coast sooner or later but are we east or west of the Panama. The storm has really slowed us down, but I can't tell how much." He took a serious drag on a cigarette and peered through the smoke at the marks he'd made on the chart over the last day. After measuring and recalculating, he threw the pencil down on the chart table. "We've got to work in closer. Maybe we can pick up some landforms on the radar that will pinpoint us on the chart. The damn LORAN is useless down here."

Scottie kept steaming southward. Periodic rain squalls engulfed us in blinding torrents of water that dissolved the distinction between sea and sky. For up to forty-five minutes at a time, cascades of water poured off the superstructure and decks. Only the sweeping eye of the radar provided visibility. The sea itself boiled with the pummeling rain which beat down the white caps but could not reduce the big swell built up by the days of high wind. When the rain let up, we strained to glimpse land below the leaden clouds. Nothing.

The hours of the afternoon crept by. Dean paced, seemingly intent on wearing a path in the steel deck. He had a depth finder on to find bottom contours. Indecision plagued him: should he turn west or east? We motored on in the growing gloom.

The radar had long since been switched to its closest range. Now and then the straight line of the shore snaked irregularly, but never definitively to correspond with a line on the chart. The depth sounder pinged from a steadily rising sea floor. As we emerged from another rain squall, we saw the land. The weak afternoon light reflected off a white line of breaking surf backed by dark jungle. Quickly, we altered course to the east to parallel the beach. The jungle glistened black green against the monotonous gray sky. Another squall hit and for fifteen minutes we were blinded by torrential rain. The squall passed and there again was the land. The surf broke violently all along the beach.

Scottie steamed on, paralleling the lee shore. The hours slipped by. Approaching night threatened before we could find the entrance to the Panama Canal. So intent were we on the nearby shore, trying to find any bit of a definitive landmark that we all jumped when Henry said: "God, there's a ship!"

Ahead, a huge black shape appeared on the horizon heading out to sea from the land. Dean madly flipped the radar to a longer range. "There it is—the ship—and the breakwaters, everything. It's the entrance to the Canal!"

We all yelled in relief. Dean pounded on the chart table. For the first time since Mobile, Henry smiled. The radar screen showed the dramatic lines of the breakwater and its maw from which the ship had steamed. The Canal was within reach.

"She's a battleship, no—could be an aircraft carrier," announced the skipper definitively. Henry was aghast and assured him it was only a big oil tanker, but the skipper would not hear of it. Another rain squall hit, obscuring everything, but when it cleared, we could see explosions of spray as waves broke along the black line of the nearest jetty. The proximity to the Panama Canal suddenly jarred the captain's memory of flag etiquette.

"Get the Panamanian flag up," Dean ordered. He had taken over the helm in the excitement of the moment. "We've got to get that flag up, so we don't have any problems when we enter the harbor." Jack and I were ordered below to a corner locker in the captain's suite.

We had not been in the captain's cabin since Mobile. Except for the lingering stench of tobacco smoke and a messy bunk, the room was still orderly despite the terrible passage. Being farther from the heat of the engine, it was distinctly cooler than our cabin.

The flags obtained in Mobile filled one locker. Rummaging head-down through the flag locker left both of us nauseated. We did not recognize the Panamanian flag by its pattern but did find the word "Panama" stenciled along the border of one of the flags. Elated, we returned to the bridge.

"Get the American flag down and that one up," ordered the captain, despite another black squall sweeping toward us.

I yanked open the port rear-facing door. The screaming wind sucked the air out of the bridge. Jack and I made our way carefully out onto the upper deck. The flag halyard was tied to the port railing and extended upward to the flag cross arm on the mast. Lashed to the halyard, a ragged American flag snapped in the shrieking wind, its streaming remnants having survived all the way from Mobile.

The wind buffeted us, its noise deafening. Spray, flung high in the air when the bow crashed through a wave, hit us like thousands of stinging bees. We clung to the guard rail, inching our way along the violently pitching deck to the point where the halyard was secured. It had been casually tied to the rail, but the days of howling wind and constant spray had set hard its knot. With each of us needing to keep one hand on the rail, neither of us could untie it. I handed the tightly folded Panamanian flag to Jack, then hooked one leg around a railing stanchion, which held me secure while I worked on the knot with both hands. It took the screwdriver blade of my Swiss Army knife to loosen the knot. We hauled down the American flag: wildly flapping red and white ribbons streaming from a torn blue field of stars. The halyard knots tied to the flag's two grommets could not be loosened and yielded only to the knife blade.

Having focused our concentration on getting the American flag down, we had lost track of an advancing rain squall until it exploded upon us. The rain came in rapid-fire cold slugs. The first torrent was so vicious it took my breath away. I could only turn my back on its fury, trying to shield my eyes in the crook of an arm. After the initial onslaught, the rain slackened just enough to allow me to open my eyes a slit. Jack was clinging to the railing with both hands, head down to the punishing rain. He had pinned the Panamanian flag to the railing in his grip. I still had one leg wrapped around the stanchion with the flapping American flag in one hand and the two ends of the wildly flailing halyard in the other. The wind yanked at both with incredible force.

"Here," I yelled while reaching out, "take this flag." He grabbed the American flag and in one unceremonious motion tucked it deep into his shorts. "OK, take one end of the halyard. Don't lose it! You tie one end of the new flag; I'll take the other."

"Right," yelled Jack. He handed me one edge of the folded flag, but it unfurled instantly and exploded into a madly snapping harpy. This flag was double the size of the American flag we'd just lowered. Jack nearly lost his grip on his corner.

Adding to the madness of the weather, the Panamanian flag had a symmetrical pattern of white and red in diagonally opposite squares, each above a star. "Damn," yelled Jack, once he had secured his grip, "which side is up?"

"I don't know!" I said, but felt the words torn from my lips. "Jack," I yelled, "let's position it with the single point of the star up."

"OK, OK," he screamed back, "let's just get it up." He was obviously not in the mood for the niceties of flag etiquette. Bundling the snapping cloth, I pinned it between the rail and my side. With Jack holding the border tight, I threaded one halyard end through a grommet and tied a bowline. We managed the same maneuver with the other grommet.

"Ready," I yelled. Jack just nodded his head in the roar of the squall. The rain, which had slackened, now intensified, coming at us in suffocating sheets.

To release the flag, I needed to step back from the railing. My plan was to untwine my leg from the stanchion and simultaneously hook one arm around the top railing. I could then use my free hand to haul on the halyard, passing it to the hand under the railing and in this way raise the flag against the force of the wind.

Just as I untwined my leg, however, a huge wave steeply pitched the deck, already deep in torrential rainwater. My feet went out from under me. My hand was yanked from the railing. I was on my hands and knees sliding backwards across the canted deck. The deep starboard roll accelerated my slide. I knew that only the starboard railing on this upper deck was between me and the engulfing sea. Was the bottom railing low enough to stop me or would I just slip under it? My buttocks slammed into the railing with marvelously reassuring pain. Still on my knees, I turned and grabbed the rail and just knelt there, shaking and staring down at the chaos of crashing wake. Then I realized the deck was nearly level, and in that instant I got up and sprinted back to Jack, who still clung to the railing, the Panamanian flag, and the halyard.

"My God, I thought you were a goner!" he yelled.

"Me too," I yelled back.

The rain suddenly stopped. From a suffocating, blinding deluge, only a few big stinging drops remained. The wind still tore at the flag, but, now able to see and on a relatively dry deck, we coordinated our efforts and had the flag flying from the yardarm in seconds.

We entered the bridge, closing the door against the raging wind. It was eerily quiet. The wind no longer ripped at our clothes, no stinging rain battered our eyes or sucked breath from our lungs. Jack and I just stood for a moment, pools of water dripping off us.

"Hey, your knees are bleeding," Henry said.

"Oh," I looked down. Blood streamed from each knee. "I fell. Had a slide across the deck in that rain squall."

"Yeah, you gotta be careful out there," said Dean, intent on steering.

Jack and I went below. Henry rummaged around and came up with a First Aid kit. Ointment and four band aids took care of the nasty-looking wounds. Dry clothing lifted our spirits. We returned to the bridge.

Tension emanated from the captain as he steered. Henry held on to the console. *Scottie* closed with the entrance to the Canal. She plowed up and over the monstrous seas that rolled past and exploded on the jetties into sheets of spray. The wind caught these great plumes and drove them over the black boulders and concrete. The gap between the massive jetties seemed small compared to the size of the seas. Very soon, *Scottie* would have to execute a 90-degree starboard turn to enter the jetties. While in that turn, she would be broadside to the angry seas.

"Damn this steering," cursed Dean. He had to turn the wheel from stop to stop before the vessel responded. "Well, we ain't got no choice. Here we go." He put the helm hard over to starboard and held it there.

Scottie turned, slowly, until she was broadside to a great sea that did not break. She lifted then dropped into a deep trough. The next towering sea formed steeply, threatening to break. We rode up its face, teetered on its unbroken top, and slid down the back side into the next trough. In slow motion, the stern came around just as the next wave broke in cascading white water that lifted *Scottie* and surfed her down its tumbling face. Dean fought the wheel, spinning it to keep the boat from broaching. The white water rushed ahead, leaving us to slide down the wave's back. The next wave did the same, but the boat managed to lift her transom high enough that the wave broke beneath us. The boat yawed wildly, but Dean managed to straighten her again while the white water rocketed us forward. The jetty wall shot past in a black blur. If we broached now, we would be on the jagged stone blocks in an instant. *Scottie* yawed and tilted down the face of the next wave, stumbling, but Dean got her bow foremost. One more wave hurtled us forward and suddenly we were in calm water with only a hint of a swell pushing us gently from the stern. It was dark. We saw the lights of Colón snaking across the black water toward us.

"We made it," whispered Henry. No bravado from the skipper; he just nodded silently. The harbor lights reflected off the sweat streaming down his face. *Scottie* swam through the still water, listing to port but safe from the storm. The land lay before us—the dark, low tropical land, barely conscious of the terrible fury just beyond the jetties.

"Where do we go now?" asked the skipper in a tired voice. He turned the helm over to Henry, then opened the Coastal Pilot shelved behind the chart table. The book described an anchorage for smaller boats on one side of the harbor. Henry pointed the boat toward a patch of black water. Dean tried the radio on a harbor frequency. A crisp voice confirmed an anchorage ahead.

Jack and I struggled with the anchor windlass for half an hour. At last, the chain rattled out through the hawse pipe. Back at the helm, Dean backed the vessel until her bow swung to the chain as the hook set. Henry went down to the engine room and shut down the main engine. The ever-present rumble was stilled. For the first time in seven days—since we left Mobile—the boat made no sound. The complete silence emphasized how greatly we had depended on the main engine. Had it failed us on the sea or coming through the breakwater, we would have perished.

Just as one of the generators coughed to life, a U.S. Customs launch came roaring across the still water. Anchoring had taken so long that Dean had had no time to prepare for this inspection. He ducked into his cabin to grab the ship's papers. Henry was still below. Jack and I ran out on deck to catch the launch's lines. The customs agent stepped on board in clean khaki pants and a pressed white short-sleeve shirt. He went straight into the galley, set his briefcase on the table, and snapped it open. Having pulled on a pair of wrinkled pants, Dean came in to greet him. His shirt was stained with sweat; a week-old beard grizzled his chin. With our grubby hair, cut-offs and t-shirts, we suspected the agent found us odorous as well.

The customs agent began by asking formal questions about where we had come from and where we were going. Dean, suddenly obsequious, added all manner of details that annoyed the official. He wanted facts about the size of the vessel for calculating the canal transit fee. Dean could not immediately answer his questions and was reduced to shuffling through a sheaf of disorganized boat papers.

"Hey," we heard from the engine room, "what's going on here?" I poked my head around the corner and saw a Latin youth half-way down the engine room ladder and Henry looking up at him from the bottom step. Jack looked up the main passage and saw another young man, having come in from the side door under the bridge, trying to push open the door to the captain's cabin. The launch crew was swarming over our vessel.

"Hey, where are you going?" Jack yelled at the one trying the captain's cabin door. There was a long silence.

"Ah, food—sandweech—you have sandweech?" came the reply.

"No, no sandwich and get away from that door!" commanded Jack.

The guy dived out the side door through which he entered. Jack locked the outer door. I went forward to lock our cabin door but had to be satisfied with hiding our valuables as we had never received a key.

Back in the galley, I found Jack telling the agent and the captain that the launch crew was invading the boat under the pretense of finding food in such places as the captain's cabin and the engine room.

"On the bigger ships, they get a handout. The water taxi service doesn't pay much and the crews often get a tip in the form of food," explained the agent.

"Sure, we can handle that," said Dean, capitulating instantly to any suggestion from the customs agent. "Make these men up some sandwiches," he ordered.

Had the agent looked up, he would have realized he was in danger of bodily injury. Jack's white pallor glowed red. The veins stood out on his temples. The strain of the voyage, the punishing seas, sleep deprivation, near capsize, the uncertainty of navigation, and now catering to a piratical launch crew focused Jack's rage on the two pompous authoritarians sitting at the galley table. Mutiny, in that instant, was in the air.

"Jack," I said, quietly pulling him into the companionway, "Jack, we can slap some cheese on the old bread we've got left. Let's just humor the skipper a bit longer."

"Humor him!" Jack said, the words hissed through clenched teeth.

"Jack, come on. Let's just use up the old bread and the Velveeta and get these guys off the boat."

"Christ, we haven't had a decent thing to eat in days and we have to feed half the thieves in Panama first," he said despairingly.

Back in the galley, I unwired the reefer and handed the bread and Velveeta to Jack. He stood at the counter and mechanically slapped one slice of cheese between two pieces of bread, heaping them on a platter he'd extracted from the dish cabinet. When the pile of sandwiches reached a perilous height, he opened the aft deck door and handed them out into the darkness. Hands grabbed the platter. Jack slammed the water-tight door and meticulously dogged each latch.

The agent proceeded to measure parts of the vessel himself, as Dean had still not come up with the ship's dimensions. When the agent returned to the galley, Henry pointed out we had autopilot and steering problems. He requested that we get dockside for repairs. The agent instructed us to radio the port captain to request a dockside birth. He also counseled us to contact our shipping agent as soon as possible. Dean had the shipping agent's number and went immediately to the bridge to use the radio. He returned to the galley in a few minutes, announcing that our agent had arranged a berth for us. The customs agent showed surprise, as dock space was often limited in Colón.

"Well," said Dean, "I'm glad to get a berth. We had a rough trip."

The customs agent gathered his papers and neatly arranged them in his briefcase. "I'm not surprised," he said dryly. "Worst storm here in ten years. Ran a freighter up on the beach west of here. Did you see it?"

"No, we had our hands full just finding the entrance through the damn rain squalls," said Dean. "We saw the warship that came out."

"I don't recall any warships lately, but you were lucky to get through the breakwater in this pumpkin. By the way, why are you flying the Panamanian flag? The Canal is U.S. territory, and you are a U.S. vessel."

"Oh, ah, yeah," said Dean, "we had it up when we were running along the coast but, of course, we don't need it now. Boys, go up and cut that rag down."

Rage, like a hot knife, seared through my fatigue. Jack recognized the red flush in my face. He seized my arm.

"You've still got your knife handy? Let's get a bit of air and cut that flag down." He dragged me unceremoniously from the galley.

"That son-of-a bitch," I said. "Look at my knees. We both could have been killed putting up that flag and he acts like it was just an oversight."

"I know how you feel, but we've got to control ourselves and get off this boat."

The agent emerged from the deck house, crossed the deck, and climbed onto the launch. The boarding party followed. Henry and Dean untied their mooring lines. The launch roared away over the calm, black water, its lights soon melding with those of Colón. The Panamanian flag, which not long ago had flapped with the fury of a tethered raptor, hung motionless. I cut it down, folding the dripping cloth while Jack re-hoisted the ragged Stars and Stripes. Its tattered condition not only testified to the wrath of the storm but also symbolized the frayed status of our nerves.

No sooner had we stepped back into the bridge when the main engine grumbled back to life. Henry fussed over the balky anchor windlass and got it working. The flukes of the anchor came up caked with sticky ooze. Still listing, *Scottie* made her way across the inky water to the docks. Working along under the shadowy transoms of the world's shipping, we found our berth across

The Panamanian flag saved from the *Scottie*. Photo courtesy of the author

from a big Norwegian freighter. As we maneuvered in, a van roared out onto the lighted dock. Ten Panamanians jumped out of it. Dry and well-clothed, these longshoremen were prepared to berth a ship. Laughter broke out amid looks of disdain and deprecating gestures as our tiny vessel nosed up to massive pilings. To add to our aggravation, Jack and I struggled to free the stern line from its multiple lashings around the lube oil drums still on deck. The boat was finally tied up; the deck gang climbed back into the van and roared away.

Again, the main engine went silent. A gust of wind swirled around the stern of the Norwegian freighter and rain spat erratically from the black sky above the dock lights. The boat was motionless. Jack and I sat on the main hatch. The humid night air was hot, but the absence of shrieking wind and threatening seas was a relief. Odors from the nearby town drifted over us. The land controlled here, not the sea. The land brought the officious customs agent, the thieves from the launch, and the snobbery of the longshore gang. The sea's power was immense but indiscriminate.

"I wonder," mused Jack, after a long silence, "if the shower works?"

"Let's try it. A shower would be miraculous."

We dove into the deck house. To our utter amazement, Henry rooted about in the galley, creating a meal. Potatoes boiled in a big pot. A huge lump of hamburger sweated toward defrost in the oven.

"Hamburgers, mashed potatoes and vegetables," he announced with delight, rummaging through the chaos in the pots and pans locker. Dean was nowhere to be seen.

"A real meal!" said Jack. "Henry, you are a genius. Do you think we could try the shower before we eat?"

"Sure, nothing wrong with it that I know of," he said, "except the water will be hot as hell from the engine room."

So it was, but just tolerable enough to allow a good soaping and duck-in-and-out rinsing. Despite its temperature, a shower had never felt so good. We donned clean clothes, an act of easy dressing impossible just hours before. Tempting aromas wafted from the galley. My appetite, hibernating during the days of constant sickening motion, awakened as in an emaciated bear. The captain burst from his cabin and headed for the galley. Jack and I fell into lockstep behind him.

"Damn, what are you cooking up, Henry, a banquet?" asked Dean.

"Just hamburgers, potatoes, and some vegetables," Henry answered, flipping patties in a large frying pan.

The galley table was neatly set. Bowls of steaming vegetables and mashed potatoes sat mid-table, not sliding from side to side. Dean said nothing but slid into his spot, with Jack and I taking ours. Henry placed the last sizzling patty on a heaped platter, set the platter ceremoniously on the table, threw the spatula into the sink, and joined us. The food was unpretentious but delicious. The galley, with the added heat of cooking, was sweltering in the tropical night, yet the meal was a banquet, an exquisite feast that only the hunger from long days at sea can prepare. We ate silently with determination that only flagged with over-satiation. Then we sat back, each contemplating the joy of eating free from the torment of constant, violent motion.

Jack and I were assigned to clean up. This night the chore was easy. Back in our cabin, we opened the ports. No firehose of spray blasted in. Instead, the cat's paws of wind swirling around the piers wafted in, relieving the heat. A light rain shower passed and cooled the humid air. We changed the bed sheets, which were stiff with salt spray and sweat. Lying in our bunks in the darkness, we considered our situation.

The five-day voyage had taken nearly eight. The memory of Mobile seemed light years in the past. The autopilot needed repair. The captain's judgement and navigational skills were, at minimum, suspect. Back in Portland, the winter quarter had begun. We had not read a page since leaving Mobile. The rest of the voyage from Panama to San Diego, where we could easily catch a flight to Portland, would take a week if all went well. The time in Colón to make repairs was unknown. The conclusion was to jump ship in Panama.

The money earned to date would have to pay the airfare. We needed to call Bill to tell him of our plan and the reasons behind it. The call needed to be made as soon as possible so he could find replacements. The problem was where to find a phone to make the call. We did not want Dean or Henry to know until the last minute, so that we could leave the boat with minimum unpleasantness. With the plan set, sleep swept over us.

CHAPTER XV
THE PORT OF COLÓN

The first hazy consciousness early Sunday morning registered a van's noisy arrival dockside, a door slamming, and another opening. Someone was rummaging loudly through tools. All this sound came in the open porthole. It dawned on me that this van had stopped at the *Scottie*.

"That must be the repair guy," said Jack sleepily. "Damn, it's only seven."

"We better see what's up," I said, getting slowly out of the bunk. Sun shone in the port and it was already hot, but this had been the first real sleep in days. I still felt I could fall back to sleep in an instant.

All four of us, looking tired, arrived in the passageway at the same time. Jack and I were sent aft to open the lazarette hatch. The sky was cloudless; the sun beat down on the deck, turning the night's shallow pools of rainwater to steam. Despite the early hour, the exertion of unlatching the hatch squeezed beads of sweat from my forehead. Henry and the repairman stood by. As soon as we lifted the hatch to one side, they descended into the shadowy lazarette. Within minutes, Henry's voice rang metallically from the steel cavern.

"Get Dean!" he commanded with urgency. The captain followed me back to the open hatch.

"Better climb down here and take a look at this," said Henry. Dean huffed down the ladder. Kneeling, Jack and I peered into the shadowy compartment.

"You see," said Henry, "the starboard steering ram is jammed under the rudder quadrant. Look here, it's bent." Then Henry stooped and picked up a large nut and not far from it, a pin. "This nut must not have been tightened at the yard. We're just lucky the ram jammed where it did, or we'd have lost all steering."

As our eyes adjusted to the darkness, we saw where Henry pointed. The rudder quadrant was affixed to the top of the rudder post. Two large hydraulic rams, one per side, provided the power to turn the rudder. The steel shaft protruding from the starboard ram was no longer attached to the quadrant. When the big pin fell out, the steel shaft had backed off, and on the next turn of the helm, pushed forward, jamming under the quadrant. The steel shaft had bent downward but because it jammed under the quadrant, it still provided some turning force. Had it not done so, *Scottie* could have lost all steering. The mess with the ram explained the reason the boat steered so poorly for the last half of the voyage.

"Jesus," said Dean, "we're lucky we made it through the damn breakwater. No wonder I had a hell of a time controlling her."

"Good thing we didn't sail on a Friday," was Henry's haunting summary.

The repairman, who'd been focused on the autopilot box, explained to Henry that he needed two repair parts. One he had in the van; the other had to be ordered from Miami.

"It will take at least three to four days to get that part. We'll be in good shape if I get my hands on it by Friday," he said, then added, "I ain't no expert on hydraulics, but I've got a suspicion it'll take longer than that to get the ram fixed." He replaced the cover on the autopilot, gathered his tools, and left.

Dean climbed out and went straight for the radio. Jack and I followed. The high cost of losing even one day in the world of big ships kept the shipping agencies available twenty-four hours a day. Dean raised our shipping agent. Within thirty minutes, a small speedy launch motored alongside *Scottie*. A slight, immaculately dressed man of Asian descent in pressed khakis and a white short-sleeved shirt climbed nimbly over the rail. He announced that he was our agent and would help us with all details while we were in Panama. He had papers for the captain to sign. While he spoke, he kept glancing around the aft deck.

"This is a small boat. I thought your vessel would be bigger. You came from Mobile in this and in such bad weather," he said as we ushered him into the galley.

Dean signed the papers, explaining the diagnosis from the autopilot repairman.

"But we have big problems with the hydraulic steering ram," he added. "We need the best hydraulics guy in Panama."

"I can get a top hydraulics guy, but not until tomorrow," said the agent. As the agent replaced the signed papers neatly in a slim briefcase, Jack stepped forward.

"Is there a phone available?" he asked.

"Yes, I can show you to the ITT office if you care to join me," he said.

"Dean, I'm willing to give Bill a call to tell him we're in Panama, but that we need repairs," Jack said. The offer was a stroke of genius. Dean was happy to let someone else call Bill and break the bad news about further delays.

"Good idea," said Dean, in his official captain's voice, "and tell Bill what a pounding we took getting the boat this far. Tell him we will have a report on the steering ram tomorrow and that I hold the yard responsible for all the repair costs."

When I asked, the agent agreed to take both of us, but recommended that we dress in the more customary long pants. We changed and in a matter of moments were aboard the launch, skimming along past the piers with ships' transoms towering above us. The launch turned between a set of piers and slowed, coming alongside a dock crowded with water taxis. Here were larger craft like the one that had transported the customs agent and the "pirates" to the *Scottie*. The shipping agent led us up the bustling dock gangway into the streets of Colón.

We passed sturdy, two-story stucco colonial buildings. This portion of Colón, the agent explained over his shoulder as we hurried along, had been the administrative center during construction of the Canal. Jack and I struggled to keep pace with the man. We were both sweating profusely. The street swayed. The feeling was so profound, that I asked the agent if this section was on piers, but he assured me that the town here was on solid ground. Rounding a corner, we came upon a sign: "ITT." The agent said goodbye and hurried off.

Inside, against one wall, was a row of wooden phone booths, each with an extension phone without a dial. A girl sitting behind a bank teller-style counter explained in heavily accented English how the system worked. Behind her sat several operators who would place the calls, then forward them to the booths. Jack wrote Bill's phone number and country information on a slip of paper. The girl directed us to an open booth and took the slip to an operator.

The office was noisy and hot. Jack sat in the booth and pulled its articulated door closed to muffle the noise. I felt the room rock under my feet. Nausea enveloped me, so I sat down on a wooden bench across the room from the booths. The phone in Jack's booth rang; he lifted the receiver and began to talk. His hair, damp with sweat, stuck to his forehead. The color drained from his face. Suddenly he hung up and struggled with the articulating door. He yanked it open and dashed across the office into the street. As I chased after him, I was terrified that the call had been a disaster. I found him sitting on the curb, head between his knees.

"Hell," he moaned when I plopped down beside him, "thought I was going to throw up in that stinking booth."

"Jack," I said, "we're land sick. This whole place feels like it's moving. We've been bouncing around for so many days on the ocean we're having trouble adjusting to solid ground."

"Amazing," he said, looking up and wiping the sweat from his forehead with the tail of his shirt. "The claustrophobic booth made it worse."

After ten minutes his nausea eased. Cautiously, we re-entered the stuffy ITT office. The call went through again. Bill agreed we should fly back. With Christmas over, he'd have no problems finding a replacement crew. He was not pleased, however, at having the boat delayed in Panama.

We left the ITT office elated. We had achieved a definitive end to the voyage, or so we thought. Bill told us to meet the shipping agent the next day to arrange the earliest flight possible for us to come home.

"Rather frustrating to come all this way, paying our dues in the storm, and not make the Canal transit," Jack observed as we walked back to the piers.

"Does seem a waste if you think about it," I agreed. "On the other hand, few have had the experience we had in just getting here."

"Few would have wanted that experience either, especially if you told them in advance what they were in for," Jack retorted.

"Would you trade it?" I asked.

"No, not now," he answered.

In that instant, the sun burst from behind the dissipating clouds, the sky turned deep blue, and the once-dull street became vibrant with colors. Steam swirled up from storm puddles. A little confused about our location, but knowing the pier number, we caught a cab back to the *Scottie*.

The boat listed to port, leaning against the pier, still catching her breath after the punishing voyage. Otherwise, she looked no worse for wear. On board, the galley was clean with a pot of coffee percolating on the stove. The washer and dryer were humming away. Henry had repaired the toilet seat. The captain had tidied up the bridge and the chaos of his chart table. All charts were rolled and stored in the overhead rack, except the one of the Panama Canal. The wounds to the railing around the chart table were still evident, along with the jury-rigged crucifix of a binnacle light above the compass. How could this very deck have tilted so far that the captain became a bowling ball, knocking Jack's legs out from under him and depositing both of them in a heap on the far side of the bridge? Compared to a square-rigger sailor waving about on a yard arm fifty feet above a wave-swept deck, ours was a trifling experience. Later we would have a hard time explaining the intensity and peril of this storm at sea. The old sailors surely experienced this dilemma, having known a reality that landlubbers could not comprehend. Little wonder the old salts were never at home on the land and preferred their own kind for friendship.

The captain proposed a celebratory toast when Jack reported he'd told Bill of the tough passage and detailed the needed repairs. Jack said nothing of our plans.

"Shore leave tonight for all," Dean announced, "with all expenses on my tab."

He had no "tab" but contacted the shipping agent on the radio, citing the delay to arrange a company draw. "I'll pick up the money on my way into town right after lunch," he concluded.

Henry, included in the plan with us, did not share the captain's jovial mood. He was more subdued than in Mobile. We'd all been in the jaws of disaster. *Scottie* could have foundered if fate had chosen. Or maybe he was reflecting on his terrifying experience swinging from the cargo hook on a stormy Caribbean night.

Shortly before the shipping agency closed, we caught a cab into town. The captain was all in white. He'd even taken time to iron immaculate creases into his white duck trousers. This touch explained the purchase of the steam iron in Mobile. A pair of white buck shoes, held in reserve, completed his formal attire, nearly duplicating merchant marine standard. The taxi, driven by a stout cabbie, wound into the drab town just awakening from the somnolence of the tropical afternoon.

"This reminds me of that place in Mexico," Dean said, half turning from his front seat. "We had a great time there didn't we, Henry?"

The cabbie drove on and on. Before leaving us at the ITT office that morning, our agent had pointed out the building housing their offices. We knew what it looked like and had a sense of its neighborhood. Although we were driving up and down streets near the agency, we came no closer to it. At last Jack, spotting the building, interrupted the captain, and ordered the cabbie to take us directly there. The cabby played dumb, but not dumb enough to miss pointing out a one-way arrow that prohibited him just then from turning in the direction we needed to go. He also made quite a fuss in broken English when we ordered him to stop the cab so we could walk the remaining blocks directly to our destination.

The tropical dusk was quickly turning to night. Dean grew concerned that the agency office would close before we arrived. When Henry found an alley that promised a short-cut, we plunged in, although it was dark and unpaved. Henry was in the lead; I followed, then came Dean with Jack bringing up the rear.

In the fading light, Henry just saw the big puddle and its narrow point which he managed to bridge in a surprisingly nimble leap.

"Watch out for the puddle," he said without turning his head.

Being next and forewarned, I had no problem clearing the puddle. Dean must have been aware of my jump. He too made it across, but Jack was behind Dean and did not hear Henry's warning. He came upon the black puddle suddenly, making an ill-prepared leap which landed his leading foot short of dry land. There came a splash, followed by a howl from the captain. As soon as we reached the streetlight at the end of the alley, we saw the black mud that peppered the back of the captain's pristine white pants.

"Damn, damn, look at this mess. All you had to do was step over the puddle. Damn it to hell."

Jack, whose foot had launched this spectacular fusillade, had mud on his shoe but otherwise appeared to have escaped the splash. No one dared speak as we hurried the last few yards to the shipping agency office.

Inside the building, we followed signs to the office on the second floor. On the way, we passed a bathroom. Dean went in, ordering Henry to pick up the cash advance.

The agency office was dominated by a large open room. Big ceiling fans rotated gracefully overhead, gently moving air around the interior. Many of the glassless windows remained shuttered following the storm, but a breeze filtered through their louvers. Streetlights glowed through the few open windows. The room was furnished with dark wooden desks, evenly spaced, which added to the sense of calm, cool order. The office had a gracious aura from another era.

Henry spoke to the sole clerk in the office, making it plain that the cash draw was in the name of the *Scottie*'s captain. Dean joined us from the bathroom. His pants were wet but clean.

"Had to take them off and wash 'em in the sink," he announced loudly to Henry, who was waiting at a counter. The clerk realized this was the captain who had demanded a draw on a Sunday afternoon and who was keeping him late while washing pants in the lavatory sink. Dean, oblivious to the clerk's disdainful mood, signed for the money, hastily thumbed through the bills, and stuffed them into a pocket.

"You best be careful, Captain," advised the clerk, locking up the cash drawer. "Colón is a rough town."

"Oh, sure," answered Dean knowingly, "I've been in a few ports in my time." He turned and headed for the stairs. As we stood in the street, awaiting a cab that the clerk had ordered for us, the last of the agency lights went out.

"Boy, we just got there in time," crowed Dean, "Now we've got some cash for a good meal."

The cab came. Dean instructed the cabby to drop us at "a good bar where we can get a cold beer and have some fun." The cabby winked. His

Chevy, complete with a large pair of white dice dangling from the rear-view mirror and a dash-mounted magnetic Madonna, swung into a maze of narrow streets.

The architecture became ramshackle, with two-story wooden structures crowded together. Some had formerly ornate second-floor balconies that now sagged unevenly and wore peeling paint. The stench of sewage wafted through the cab's open windows. Christmas lights hung randomly across one intersection, an anomaly in the January tropical heat. Henry liked the balconies and said they expressed the Spanish penchant for overlooking the evening promenade. He envisioned black-laced beauties with fans, haughtily yet keenly viewing the men in the street.

The cab dropped us in a block with gaudily decorated bars pulsing in a chaos of neon lights. A half-starved dog wandered by. A toothless old man in a tattered tank-top stared at us from a crooked doorway. He gummed something in the black cavity of his mouth. Music blasted through speakers directed onto the street from the bars, creating a cacophony matching the chaos of lights. The captain obsessed about picking "the right bar," as though one differed substantially from another. Suddenly he dived into one; its portly barker ushering us in quickly before we changed our minds.

The establishment consisted of two rooms. The outer, smaller one was decorated with a hodgepodge of tasseled plastic paintings—Heineken and Coca Cola advertisements. Several customers lined the bar itself, huddled in conversation over their drinks. When we entered, they all stopped talking to stare long and hard at the newcomers.

The bar barker, now transformed into our best friend, began a running dialogue in broken English. The best drinks and companionship were in the second room. He held aside the stings of beads in the inner doorway so we could enter the second, larger room. At one end, on a small stage, a band was just setting up. The room was packed with tables and chairs, but we were the only customers. A tight knot of young women sat talking around a table near the stage. They looked up, surprised at the arrival of new customers so early in the evening, but the commanding snap from the barker's fingers brought them fluttering. A cloud of cheap perfume engulfed us. They giggled, grabbed our arms, and pulled us to "a table at the front for my friends," as instructed by their boss.

The women seated us and pulled in their chairs, hemming us in. Each one was dark-skinned, with black hair, but wore thick make-up to lighten their faces. One—a Columbian, as she proudly told us—could speak English.

The captain was in his glory, puffed like a male peacock by the mere proximity to so many cooing females. He ordered a round of drinks with a flourish. The astronomical cost of each drink explained why the barker was so quick and happy to accommodate the captain's request. The scotch for the captain and engineer, and beer for Jack and me, were genuine; the champagne ordered for the ladies was ginger ale. The captain quietly proposed that I buy the next round. Jack's disdain for our female companions was growing along with his annoyance at the captain's vices.

The band began playing with an ear-shattering blast. The cacophony left Henry gulping scotch as an anesthetic. Jack leaped up, excusing himself. I followed. The captain, who viewed Jack as Bill's spy on this trip, protested perfunctorily but in fact seemed relieved to be rid of him and of me, too. The women felt differently. They clung to us tightly. After we pried ourselves free and left the room, two followed us to the outer door, imploring us to stay for a little fun. We bolted into the relative safety of the street. Walking away from the bar, however, we were quickly hailed by a pimp who had witnessed our harried escape from the bar.

"Yeah, them no good," was his opening line. "Ugly, fea, yeah, but I know some beauties, racehorses, just right for young bucks like you," his sing-song tone had a Caribbean rhythm. When it became obvious that we were not buying, his voice became a weapon filled with invective, yelling "no cojones" as we scurried around the nearest corner. One step off the main street, the darkness of the tropical night was nearly complete. We stopped, breathing hard, unable to proceed until our eyes adjusted to the dark. Fear, like a stench, seeped up through the mud of the street. We peered back around the corner. The pimp had melted into the night crowd on the narrow sidewalk. We darted out of the foul-smelling side street and hailed a cab. Back on board, the *Scottie* had become a quiet haven.

The beer, the numbing volume of the band, the oppressive heat, and the suffocating humidity created a throbbing headache. Jack complained of one also. We found a snack and aspirin. Fatigue drove us to our bunks. Open portholes and an open cabin door produced little cross-ventilation. Jack set up the little fan, but it hardly stirred the molasses-like air.

I awoke suddenly in the middle of the night, sitting upright in my bunk. Sweat poured down my face. The dock light shown through the porthole. *Scottie* was tied safely to the dock, but a nightmare had taken me back to a night in Johnstone Strait, to when I had been returning on the *Susan Ann* from my first season of commercial salmon fishing in Southeast Alaska.

At the beginning of the season when we were loading our personal gear onto the *Susan Ann* docked in Anacortes, I had set my two duffle bags down on the dock. One of the bags, zipped shut, contained my personal gear. The other contained my diving gear, and the new big fins I had just purchased did not allow me to zip the bag shut.

"You a diver?" asked a voice from behind me.

"Well, I can dive," I said, turning around.

"You a crew on the *Susan Ann?* First time up?" The speaker was an old guy with a gray stubble.

"Yes."

"Unless you are a professional diver, I would leave that stuff at home," he said.

"Well, the skipper asked me to bring it along."

"Just what I thought," he said and walked away.

Just after midnight, Rob stood at the bow of the *Susan Ann* with a spotlight. On our way home from Ketchikan, we had entered the northern end of Johnstone Strait only to find it packed with night-fishing gillnetters. Hundreds of dim lights were scattered across the inky dark waters. Each boat had a single white light on board and one slightly dimmer white "pot" light at the end of their net. We needed to get through the strait without snagging a net in our prop. We had to guess which white light was the boat and which white light was the net that went with that boat, selecting one end or the other to round.

In the darkened bridge, the skipper hunched over the wheel with the boat running nearly at idle. I was on the starboard side of the bridge and Rob on the port side. For a long while we guessed right, until—

"Cork line!" yelled Rob, and his spot shown on a line of corks that disappeared under the bow. The skipper pulled the throttle and shift lever to neutral.

"Run back and see if we slide over it," the skipper commanded.

We ran back with a flashlight in time to see the cork forming a V trailing into our dark wake.

"Shit, the prop must have still been wind-milling. We snagged this one," Rob yelled up toward the bridge.

Mel arrived at the stern. We heard the engine of a gillnetter start nearby and saw a white light heading for us.

"Looks like we snagged you," yelled Mel.

A small guy at the outside wheel of the gillnetter stepped into the circle of his deck light, looking at the net trailing aft of the much larger *Susan Ann*.

"Yep," said the gill net guy. "I'll get a hold of the net on this side and give a tug. Maybe it will come free."

"Yeah," said Mel, "I had her in neutral. Maybe it snagged on just one of the flukes."

The gillnetter worked in close, picking up a section of his cork line and attempted to reel it onto his drum, but it did not budge.

"Got that wet suit of yours?" Mel asked.

"Yes, but I don't have an air tank," I said.

"Better go get it on. I am hoping you can get it off with just a free dive," Les said. "We are drifting now until we get untangled from this guy, and I am not sure how far we are offshore."

I got into the wet suit and strapped on the weight belt, knowing I would need it to get to neutral buoyancy. At the stern rail, I looked down into the black water.

"I don't have a light," I said.

"We'll shine our spotlight aft and the gillnetter says he has one he'll shine into the water when you are ready. We have rigged a line so you can lower yourself down."

I spit into my mask to keep it from fogging, slipped it on, and put its attached snorkel into my mouth. I then made my way to the rail, flip-flopping in my big new fins. I was able to use the rope a bit to go down, but the fins were hopeless on the side of the boat so I fell into the water more than lowering myself into it. I had the presence of mind to hold the mask to my face but the rush of icy water into my wet suit burned like a hot knife. My head had gone under, so when I surfaced I blew the water from my snorkel. Swimming a few strokes aft, I peered down. The light from the spots disappeared into bottomless, terrifying blackness. Whatever was down there could see me but I could not see it.

Taking a deep breath through the snorkel, I dived under the stern counter. The propeller was deeper down than I had imagined, and the gillnet was looped around it. I grabbed the cork line and attempted to lift if off an upper fluke but I could not move it. The line had made one loop around the flukes.

"Give me the knife," I yelled when I got to the surface and got the snorkel out of my mouth. "There's a loop around the prop and I can't free it. I have to cut it."

A big knife was handed down to me by a body held by its legs. Clearing my snorkel again, I took several deep breaths, held the last one, and swam downward toward the blackness. Keeping my eyes on the curve of the hull until I got to the prop, I began sawing on the rope. The rope was surprisingly tough and I worked on it as long as my breath lasted, but had to return to the surface. Again I blew the water out of the snorkel, and breathed deeply several times before holding the last big breath. Below, after long seconds, I found the cut spot in the rope and went to work again. Just as I was running low on air, the knife blade went through and I turned up for the surface.

Suddenly the net was all around me and raked the mask off my face. I tried to reach up to replace it, but the net had drifted down around my shoulders. I could not move my arms to reach the mask and was nearly blind. I kicked. My fins and legs were still free and I began to move upward, but slowly. I kicked harder and my lungs burned. I was moving up but too slowly. I suddenly realized I could reach the buckle on my weight belt and tore at it until the belt dropped from my waist. Now I moved up more rapidly, kicking consistently with the big fins. My lungs burned. My thoughts were very clear: the only thing you can do until the end is keep kicking as hard but as steadily as you can. Shit, I had to breathe. My whole body was on fire. I would not make it.

Suddenly, net and all, my head broke the surface. Somehow I remembered to spit out the snorkel mouth-piece and gasped. Sweet air filled my lungs. I gasped again and again, still kicking to keep my net-draped head clear of the sea.

"There he is! Over there!" I heard someone shout. "He's caught in the net. Pull it over here!" Then I felt the net begin to tow me toward the *Susan Ann* and soon I was alongside. I could not speak but just kept breathing in and out and kicking upwards.

"Give us your hands," said someone.

"I can't, they're caught in the net," I blurted out.

The net jerked upwards. Then it came off my head and soon I was clear of it. I reached up and someone grabbed my hand. I was hauled halfway up the hull and felt other hands grabbing my shoulders and under my arm pits and I was flopped over the rail like a tuna. I just lay there for a moment, feeling the fresh air in my lungs.

"You OK?" someone asked.

"Yeah . . . but the net came over my head . . . didn't think I was going to make it."

"I told you he was down too long," said Rob accusingly.

After a moment I said, "I got the cork line cut through, so haul on it and it should come free."

I heard the gillnetter's engine and then a whoop as the net cleared our stern.

For a long while I sat upright at the galley table before attempting to take off my wet suit.

And then I was back on the *Scottie*, sitting upright in my bunk. In the nightmare, I had experienced the same piercing clarity of thought as when *Scottie* lay shuddering on her side.

LOGBOOK, DAY 10: JANUARY 12, 1970

In the dark hours of Monday morning, a commotion dockside awakened me. The sound of voices filtered through the open port—the laugh of a woman and Henry's slurred tones. I was dozing again when the patter of footsteps on the deck outside our cabin brought me wide awake. Suddenly a woman's head popped in through the open porthole, surveyed my semi-nude form from head to foot, then disappeared. Another head greatly resembling our engineer appeared at the port. The head with Henry's voice mumbled a tipsy apology for interrupting anyone's sleep and explained that the *Scottie* was hosting a couple of young ladies. Then this face withdrew, carried away by padding footsteps.

"Visitors," I said to the darkness.

"Great," said Jack from below, "just great. It's not bad enough, this insufferable heat, but now we can't escape the captain's parties."

The galley filled with low tones, loud hissing whispers, and the slamming of a door as the party moved inside. Drawers and cabinets were opened and slammed shut. The refrigerator door was opened and banged shut repeatedly. A woman's high-pitched laughter pierced the muffled discussions. Jack groaned. The sound of voices dissipated; doors closed. After a few moments, the silence was broken by the sound of water from the shower. A door opened and closed. Bodies padded along the inside passage. We had closed our cabin door when the party boarded, eliminating the chance of a breeze. Silence returned, leaving the suffocating heat and the annoying glare of the dockside light through the open port.

I abruptly awakened from fitful dozing. Night still gripped the vessel. My heart pounded in the awareness that somebody had entered our cabin. As my eyes focused, I made out the figure just inside our cabin door. For an instant, the form stood still. The droplets of sweat popped out along my forehead. Where had I put my Swiss Army knife? The form suddenly stepped out of the shadow and became a dark-skinned girl wrapped in a white towel. She leaned forward, peering curiously into the shadows of Jack's bunk, the towel forming around her firm, ample breasts.

"Hold it, you've got the wrong cabin," said Jack clearly.

This sudden pronouncement from the darkness of the lower bunk startled her. She jumped back involuntarily, but when nothing else happened, she straightened, put a hand deliberately on a curvaceous hip and said, "No, me right!"

"Look, you've got the wrong cabin. Clear out of here now."

"I no go," she said in a pouting voice, the words slightly slurred from alcohol.

Now that she was standing upright, she could see across my bunk's lee board. She stared at my prone figure lit by the dockside light. I had hoped to escape detection by lying perfectly still. She stepped forward, resting her elbows on the bunk board.

"Who you?" she inquired.

"Ah, just crew," I answered, growing uncomfortable under her unabashed scrutiny. Her face was not beautiful but not ugly either.

"Ha," she said both triumphantly and disdainfully. "You no big shot."

For an instant I wondered what she, after reviewing my exposed body, had meant exactly. She talked so loudly that I was more concerned about avoiding a row than clarifying what she was talking about.

"No, no big shot," I agreed in a whisper.

She reached languidly over the edge of the bunk and ran a warm hand over my chest. Quickly, she tried to pinch my left nipple.

"No," I said, in a plain voice, rolling away from her. All I needed now was the captain to enter, especially if she was his girl for the night. My quick movement brought a flash of anger from her.

"I older than you," she said, stamping a bare foot on the deck, "I eighteen. How old you?"

Now I felt suddenly sorry for her. She had probably just rolled out of the sack with the captain, a man over twice her age. Maybe all her lovers had been as old and as disloyal.

"I'm twenty-one," I whispered in the faint hope this would avoid more loud talk.

"No you not!" she said with conviction but in a whisper too. "Besides, I have two babe," she added triumphantly.

Suddenly I was aware of a whole class of women living in the reeking back streets of Colón seeking escape from poverty by grabbing at the human flotsam and jetsam of the world's transient seamen. I said nothing.

"I bed with you," she announced, attempting to hoist herself up into my bunk.

"No," I said forcefully. She was too drunk to swing up into my upper berth.

"Oh, then I go with him," she said defiantly, angrily, and she rolled into Jack's lower bunk.

Suppressing laughter, I rolled to the edge of my bunk, peering into the darkness below to see how Jack, who had been so quiet, was going to handle this hot potato. I could see the white patch of her towel which must have come off, as it was draped over the side of the lower bunk. All was quiet for an instant, then Jack came vaulting out of the bunk.

"No," he commanded, standing in his white undershorts. "Get out of here. Come on, get out before you get us all in trouble." As he spoke, he hauled the protesting girl by the arm from his bunk. She was naked, so he handed her the towel quickly, then ushered her to the door. She had a beautiful shape. Jack was taking no chances. He moved her, despite a stream of protest in Spanish, steadily out the door, which he closed quickly and locked. She fell silent and did not attempt to re-enter.

"I don't believe it." I burst into laughter.

Jack stood, slump-shouldered, slowly shaking his head back and forth.

"Come to think of it, without the shadow of the captain at the door or you in that upper bunk, I may not have been able to throw her out."

Later that morning, I woke to the sun well above the horizon. Heat swam into the tiny cabin through the port. A wickedly distended bladder got me out of the bunk. I scrambled to unlock the door and checked that the passage was clear, then dashed for the head. To my surprise, the head door was locked. In distress, I knocked. No response; not a sound. Wasting no time, intending to pee off the stern, I hurried back to the cabin, pulled on my cut-offs and boots and scampered out on deck. To my dismay, the dock was a beehive of activity with a big freighter coming in and the longshoremen milling about, ready to handle the lines. Too many eyes to witness my piss off the stern. I ran around to the head porthole, peering in to see if someone had passed out within. The room was empty. I thought momentarily of climbing through the porthole, but in my condition the added pressure as I wiggled through could be fatal. I turned to pee off the starboard railing, but opposite was the large Norwegian freighter with several people at the rail watching the activities on our pier. I could not pee here either. My increasing pain demanded unlocking the head door.

Frantically, I banged on the captain's door. We had never locked the head door. The skipper had invited company onboard, and he had the keys. I pounded on the door so unmercifully that I roused Jack, who poked his head out our cabin door. The captain finally responded and opened the door.

"What's up?" He was groggy.

"The damn head door is locked from the inside. No one's in there. I gotta take a leak and the dock is like Grand Central. Do you have the key to the head?"

"OK, OK," he said, then shut the door.

I heard drawers opening and closing and then a jangling sound. The door opened just enough to allow his hand through, holding a fat ring of keys. I grabbed them. Every damn key to every lock onboard was there, unmarked.

Jack followed me to the head door. In a crescendo of pain, I tried every key. None worked. Jack began to try each one.

"I can't stand it, Jack. Help me through the porthole before I explode!"

With Jack providing a leg up, I got through the porthole without rupturing my bladder, even though I landed in a handstand—which to my great surprise eased the pain until I stood upright. I made it to the toilet, and during the joy of relieving my anguish, I looked up to see a pair of women's panties hanging from the towel rack.

This voyage, conceived on a late rainy evening in the spirit of Conrad and Melville, was reduced to the banality of a pair of panties. Anger seared my brain like a hot brand. We had survived the fury of the storm, tormenting winds, and malevolent seas. The land knew nothing of the ocean's indifferent savagery. The land was banality, full of temptations, betrayals, and compromises. The anger suddenly subsided. Perhaps Conrad was not dead after all. The sea was still the primal element, enforcing one clear dictum: survival.

"Are you all right?" yelled Jack, knocking on the still-locked door.

I opened the door and pointed to the panties, "There."

"Shit!" he said, "She walked out and left the door locked."

I wondered if Jack saw the other side of the issue, but before I could ask, Henry poked his head in the door.

"Well," he said, after we explained about the locked door, "I prefer the very clean type—shower and all, you know."

Soon Dean was up, convincing Henry to make another king's breakfast. Nothing was seen of the two women. Before long, the captain, in high spirits, was wielding a spatula over the hot cakes. Jack and I did not share his mood, because soon we had to announce our plan to leave the *Scottie*. After a brief consultation in our cabin, we agreed there was no better time than the present, with the captain in a jubilant mood and two ladies still aboard.

✸

Dean slammed the spatula down. Our announcement of departure caught him by surprise. When he realized that Bill had to know, he felt threatened. He was not concerned about our departure as such. New crew could be found, but our leaving could be taken as a criticism of his abilities.

"Shit," I began, in a flash of anger.

"Look," said Jack cutting me off, "we have to get back to classes as soon as possible. I told Bill that with these breakdowns, which were out of everyone's control, we have no idea when we might get back. He knows we are out of time." These arguments, especially about breakdowns beyond anyone's control, placated the captain and quelled my counterproductive anger. With a wave of the spatula, Jack and I were cleared to proceed to the shipping agent's office to finalize our plans for departure. Jack and I wasted no time, scrambling up the dock ladder to hail a cab.

The shipping agent found us two seats on a flight leaving from Panama City the following afternoon.

"Great!" we both said.

"To be sure to make the flight, you need to spend the night in Panama City," said the agent, "but to leave the vessel you have to clear U.S. Customs first. The customs agent might put you into quarantine tonight in Panama City, so you do not go anywhere else before you leave." The way he said the word "quarantine" made it sound like a prison. With the specter of incarceration weighing on us, the agent directed us to the U.S. Customs Office down the street.

The Customs Office was heavy with bureaucracy, and we felt vaguely like criminals reporting to a police precinct. We presented the paperwork prepared at the shipping agency to an officer behind a counter. He read through it, stamped a page, then instructed us to prepare our gear for immediate departure from the *Scottie*. We would spend the rest of the time before the flight in the U.S. Customs Quarantine Compound outside of Panama City. To us, this sounded like a jail sentence. Jack felt he was being categorized as a criminal, one of the riffraff of the world's merchant fleets, and a ship-jumper at that.

"Look, we're U.S. citizens," he began. I could see the color rising up his neck and flushing his cheeks.

"The regulations are the same for all seamen," snapped the customs agent.

Now it was my turn to mediate. Tangling with U.S. Customs was a more serious threat to our escape plan than a spatula-waving captain.

I pulled Jack aside. "We can manage one night in quarantine after what we've been through, and then we will be winging our way home. Lunging across the counter to throttle an agent of the U.S. government will not help us." Jack recovered his composure.

The agent dispatched us to the *Scottie* to collect our gear. Another customs agent would pick us up at the boat and transport us to the afternoon train across the Panamanian isthmus. In Panama City, a car would collect us at the station for the ride to the quarantine compound.

Outside the office, our shipping agent waited to explain how we were to collect our tickets at the Pan American airline counter at the airport. When he learned of our assignment to quarantine, he said, "Well, it just depends on the agent you get." Jack got furious again.

By noon we were back aboard the *Scottie*. The breakfast dishes were heaped in the sink. An open bottle of rum, half full, surrounded by Coke cans, dominated the galley table. Two dock hands sat behind the table, sipping their drinks and providing an audience for Dean, who regaled them with his sea stories and amorous conquests. The two young women of the previous night flitted back and forth between the captain's stateroom and the rum. Music blared from the boat's loudspeakers. Jack and I plunged through the party to our cabin, closed the door (but failed to lock it), and began to throw our belongings into sea bags. No sooner had we begun than a customs agent appeared dockside, pacing back and forth. Jack poked his head out the porthole to look, only to have the agent yell, "Hurry up!"

In the midst of our packing frenzy, the cabin door flew open and the two women, reeking of rum, barged in. We had met the one in our cabin the previous night. The other was a plump Latin woman, who appeared to be totally inebriated. When they realized we were packing, they screeched at us not to go. We ignored them—not easy in a tiny cabin—and kept packing. When we did not stop, the girls began pulling our packed clothes out of our sea bags.

"Stop!" Jack yelled.

The plump one grabbed us both by the hair. She was amazingly strong. Momentarily paralyzed by pain, I thought she was going to pull a handful of hair right out of my head. Jack freed himself first and got an arm around her throat. That hold loosened her grip on my hair. Jack rotated her towards the door, which I scrambled to open. He pushed her out, and I slammed the door, locking it. We turned for the other woman, but she threw herself into the lower bunk, cowering against the wall.

"I no problem, no problem," she pleaded. "Just stay here, no trouble."

We continued to pack. The shadow of the customs agent pacing on the dock crossed the porthole. Jack, ready to make his break, stationed himself by the door, listening for the other woman. I could not find my toilet kit, which I had dropped when attacked by the hair-puller. I looked in the lower bunk and realized that girl held it behind her head. She smiled.

"Oh, shit," I said. "She's got my toilet kit."

Jack took one look and was out the door.

She had opened the buttons of her blouse all the way to her navel, a white bra definitive against the brown firm skin of her breasts. I leaned in to grab the kit. She extended her arm, holding the kit beyond my grasp.

"Stay," she implored, pursing her lips and arching her back. I reached further into the bunk, getting a hand on the kit. Our faces now close, she brought her warm lips full onto mine. I lingered for an instant. Her grasp relaxed ever so slightly on the kit. I pulled it away; our lips parted. I staggered back, then grabbed the sea bag and dashed from all that temptation. A slight plaintive squeal followed me out the door.

I still had clothes in the dryer in the head. I'd planned to dive in to grab them, but the other woman stood in the doorway to the head, laughing. She stepped forward, reaching for my hair. I ducked past her grasp, crossing the galley. Dean stood by the sink, waving the spatula and a glass of rum. In horror, I realized the shirt he had on, the one with egg down the front, was mine.

"See you in Seattle," Dean roared happily as I bolted past, the woman pursuing me with outstretched hands. I made it to the deck, scalp intact. Behind me the galley erupted in laughter. I jammed the toilet kit into the sea bag, zipped the whole mess shut and heaved it up into Jack's waiting arms dockside. Before I scampered up the ladder, I took one last quick look at *Scottie*.

"Jesus, I barely made it off that boat," I said to Jack and the customs agent, who looked impatient and perturbed.

"We're going to miss the damn train," he said angrily. And we did. The steam locomotive was puffing away down the track as we wheeled into the train station.

"Damn, the next train ain't until 4:30," said the agent. "I'm not going to hang around here with you two 'til then." He regarded us coldly, judging us as he had undoubtedly judged many other sailors in his line of duty. "If you two can be good boys and promise to be on that 4:30 train, I can turn you loose for the next few hours. If you ain't on the train and miss the ride on the other end, then I'll make sure you're arrested; understand?"

"We'll make the next train—promise," said Jack quickly.

"I'll call ahead for the car on the other end. He'll know if you ain't on that train, and when I catch up with you, it'll be a federal offense."

"We'll be there. You won't have to worry," I said.

"I'm sure you will," he said as he jerked his thumb for us to get out.

We were leery of leaving our gear at the station, so, sea bags in hand, we trudged into Colón. The hot sun was a pile-driver pounding us into the pavement. We picked a big bar that advertised air-conditioning. Inside, our eyes struggled to adjust to the shady darkness, but it was mercifully cool. We groped our way into the dim bar, dropped the bags at the foot of some empty stools, and ordered "cold" Heinekens.

CHAPTER XVI
RETURN FROM PANAMA

And this is all that is left of it! Only a moment; a moment of strength, of romance, of glamour—of youth! . . . A flick of sunshine upon a strange shore, the time to remember, the time for a sigh, and—good-by! — Night—Good-by . . .

—Joseph Conrad, *Youth*

"I'll buy," came a voice from the shadows. The voice was unmistakably that of the engineer. Beer in hand, Henry came to join us. Our mouths fell open. Only now did it dawn on us that Henry had been absent from the *Scottie* during our escape.

"Well," he said, mounting a stool, "you made the right choice. While you were out, the hydraulics guy came aboard. Two weeks to get a new steering ram from Miami, maybe more." He tipped his glass to us. We all took a long drink. The beer was a cool sip from heaven to the parched in purgatory.

Henry, away from the *Scottie* and her manic captain, started talking. He was concerned about the skipper. Having sailed with him on many voyages, he had never seen Dean so nervous and irrational. He had accompanied Dean many summers to Alaskan waters, running salmon tenders. He talked of the power scow, the *Victor H.* In an afternoon of coincidences, this was another: When commercial salmon fishing in Kodiak, our boat unloaded fish one day to the *Victor H* tender. She was big and, as I recalled, run haphazardly with a wild crew. This fact I did not mention to Henry, who remembered Dean in better control in those days. I couldn't remember Henry or Dean from that encounter, but one doesn't see much from a seiner's hold when pitching salmon into a brailer.

The fact that Henry was sitting quietly by himself in this bar testified to his estrangement from Dean. The changes he saw in his friend saddened him. Other matters haunted him. He liked the old Spanish look in Colón and speculated on just how much it would take to "get by" south of the border. "Not a place like Colón, something a little cheaper and less rough," where he could spend a few months to put his life back together. He said he had been a pretty fair musician, but that was slipping away. He was tiring of the vagabond life with Dean, "tired of the disruptions," he said. The escapades no longer had the thrill of adventure they once held. Here was a man of multiple talents at middle age, wondering about a life beginning to ebb with little to show for it.

At one point a thick-set, heavily made-up woman walked up to Henry. Her approach was direct: she reached to unzip his fly. Craftily, he sent her on to the next seaman down the bar, who exclaimed loudly in a Cockney accent, "Twenty dollars—out of the question!"

We ordered another beer, and then another, hearing of the days when Henry was a hot young trumpeter on the way up. He had played in Harry James's band. At some point, I looked at my watch. Shit, the train was leaving in 15 minutes. Quickly, we bade Henry farewell. He wished us both the best of luck. As we rushed out, I glanced over my shoulder. I can still see him there in the cool gloom, contemplating the diminishing options of his life.

The sun hammered against our temples pulsing with cold beer as we hurried through the crushing heat and humidity toward the train station. The streets were empty except for one stray thin dog nuzzling garbage in the gutter. The verandah over the train platform shimmered before us, an oasis of shade.

Just as we hit the shade, the steam locomotive labored into view, puffing with a solid, rhythmic reliability, defying the torpor of heat and the smell of decay. The windows of the few passenger cars had no glass. Soon we were inside the last car, sitting upright on hard, straight-backed wooden seats. The engine gained speed with its quickening, chugging breaths.

The track carried us straight out of the sunlight into a lush, shadowy jungle. Great leafy plants backed by dense vines and an impenetrable riot of undergrowth reached out toward the track, waving violently in the gust of the steam engine's passage. Eventually the train broke out of the jungle, passing an open, green lawn surrounding several two-story colonial buildings:

order against the chaos of the jungle. Then the leafy plants engulfed us again. The track curved a bit and we saw, floating high above the jungle, the superstructure of a great ship. The foliage closed in again, waving.

Too soon we clattered into the station in Panama City. The engine's magnificent chant quelled to mumbled hissings. Not a government driver, but a cabby, came looking for us.

"You go to quarantine?" he asked.

"Yeah, yeah," said Jack.

Reluctantly, we piled our baggage and then ourselves into the beat-up cab. We rattled off through Panama City streets, wider and more substantial than Colón's. Jack sat sullenly looking out the window. The cab left the city, passing verdant jungle, then made a turn onto a country lane. Across wide, green lawns with great shade trees stood more white two-story colonial buildings. The cab motored into the curved drive of one with screened verandahs all around. As we unloaded, we noted the shade of the great trees. In the lobby, under a lazily turning ceiling fan, a happy Latin clerk signed us in. A smiling maid handed us crisp, clean, white sheets and towels, thick and soft.

"And here," said the clerk, after providing us with the key to our room, "is the pass to go into the city."

"What?" asked Jack.

"The pass. You eat dinner here or go into the city, but you come back here for sleep," he said, more like a hotel manager than the prison guard Jack had envisioned.

"Oh," said Jack, but not more.

We followed the maid to the second floor. She showed us to a plain but clean room with two beds, neat lockers, and a writing table with two chairs. She said we could choose another room, but this one suited us. We checked out the bathrooms at the end of the hall: clean with large showers. Huge shower nozzles gushed water under powerful pressure. After we luxuriated in their massaging spray and dressed in clean clothes, we strolled around the immaculate grounds in the tropical dusk. Cicadas chorused from the surrounding jungle. We passed only one other seaman, and he was admiring the beautiful flowers. The distinctly pleasant sensation of being transported back to another era settled over us with the darkness.

We met the seaman again in the cool portico of our building. He was Greek and about our age. His English was limited, but better than our

Greek. He had finished his stint on a merchant ship and was headed back to Greece, to his family home on an island somewhere. He had a countryman friend in Panama City who ran a small Greek restaurant. Would we join him for dinner?

Passes in hand, we caught a cab into the city. The little restaurant, on a crowded street, was not long on ambiance, except for a battered print of the Acropolis, but our new friend was greeted like a mythic hero returning home. We dined on fresh food, marvelously prepared, with the flavor of lemon and grape leaves. The chicken had a light sauce, was golden in hue, and melted on the tongue. Jack and I, who had spent most of the trip eating the *Scottie*'s restricted fare after the failure of the refrigerator doors, ate like men freed from a desert isle. Our host was pleased that we consumed the food of his homeland with such enthusiasm.

Our new friend's next passion plunged us from the sublime of the Greek food to the ridiculousness of Japanese Godzilla movies. We declined to join him for the double feature. With the cool, quiet buildings of the quarantine compound in mind, we bid him farewell and caught a cab back to our quarters.

The compound lay well beyond the noisy city and its plethora of neon; out here, stars peppered the inky black dome of night down to the horizon. The big ones seemed to pulsate. Away from the heat-retaining concrete and the grime of car exhausts, gentle night breezes played refreshingly across the lawns. All around, nocturnal insects sang out their territory.

In our tidy room, we calculated the earnings and debts from the voyage and plane fare. After paying all our costs, we would each be $25 richer. That was, given all considerations, not too bad. After we turned out the light, events of the voyage paraded across my consciousness. I felt lucky to be here in this compound. Little did I know that, in three years, *Scottie* would be at the bottom of the Bering Sea.

LOGBOOK, DAY 11: JANUARY 13, 1970

A cacophony of bird calls greeted the dawn. Vibrantly colored yellow and black birds with bright coal-black eyes swarmed in the great trees. Each was a

Caruso with a voice and ego to challenge the sun. A fresh breeze, wafting in the window, carried the scent of bacon.

After another shower, we found the dining room, where we were treated to a full breakfast including fresh-squeezed orange juice, perfectly scrambled eggs, and fluffy pancakes. The thick bacon lived up to its tantalizing

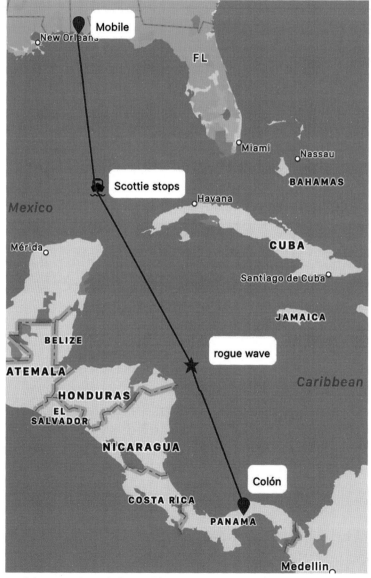

Course of the *Scottie* through the Caribbean.

scent. The fresh coffee flowed black and bountiful. Sitting on the verandah after breakfast, we realized that the time had come to depart for the airport, but we didn't want to go. In the few hours we'd spent on the train across the isthmus and in the compound, we had experienced a serene oasis apart from the hot, putrefying towns.

What followed was a day of airports, long lines, and long flights. A cab took us to the airport; from there, we flew to Miami then on to points west and north, until late that night we arrived in Portland, numb and tired.

My first class the following morning was logic. I never did well in it: whether it was the late start after the voyage or the shadow of the voyage itself, logic's abstractions lived in a universe remote from what I had just experienced. Events of the voyage came with ranks of variables, not just one or two. What about the coincidences and near fatalities and the misfortunes that the storm forced upon us? Reason could not fathom the challenges we faced. The long shadow of that sea voyage affected more than that logic class.

CHAPTER XVII
THE ROMANCE OF ILLUSION

. . . looking still, looking always, looking anxiously for something out of life, that while it is expected is already gone—has passed unseen, in a sigh, in a flash—together with the youth, with the strength, with the romance of illusions.

—Joseph Conrad, *Youth*

Back at the Veritable Quandary, Jack put down his empty glass. The waitress quickly picked it up.

"Do you want another round? I'm going off shift now and need to close your tab," she said, her tone perfunctory.

Waiting for her return, I could see that Jack was far away, as I had been. We now looked back on youth, seeking in the concentric rings of life's choices, something lost. In the tedium and safety of responsibility, the door had closed on adventure. But at least we had those experiences to remember.

EPILOGUE
LOSS OF THE *SCOTTIE*

S*cottie* sank on September 11, 1973, three and a half years after our delivery voyage. She began taking on water 16 miles northwest of Port Moller in the Bering Sea. *Scottie* issued a mayday call, reporting that water was gushing into the engine room and the boat was sinking rapidly. The crew of four abandoned ship into a rescue life raft. The U.S. Coast Guard deployed the cutter *Jarvis* and two Coast Guard aircraft were sent out from Cold Bay. The fishing vessel *Sea Spray* managed to get to the sinking site first, rescuing the four men in the life raft.

The following information is from the *Point Adams Packing Company vs. Astoria Marine Construction and the Bender Welding and Machine Company* lawsuit heard before the Ninth Circuit U.S. Court of Appeals on April 4, 1979. Point Adams was the owner of the *Scottie* at the time of the sinking. The court case describes the circumstances around the loss of the vessel as follows:

Facts:

- The *Scottie* was a ninety-foot crab fishing vessel owned by Point Adams. It was built by Bender and delivered to Point Adams in 1970. The *Scottie* was used in the Alaskan fishing waters from 1970 until it sank in September of 1973. The sinking was caused by flooding in the craft's lazarette and engine room. Water initially entered the lazarette from an unknown cause and passed through an eight-inch pipe into the engine compartment.

- The *Scottie*, and its sister vessel, the *Stevie*, were built by Bender for Point Adams in 1969. By a letter of agreement, the Point Adams—Bender construction contract was modified to include language which provided that the vessels would be built to the best commercial marine practice. Point Adams claims that this language established an express warranty and that pursuant to the express warranty, Bender should have installed a high-water alarm in the lazarette. This alarm would have provided an early warning that water had entered the lazarette.

- In April of 1973, the *Scottie* was taken to Astoria Marine Construction's shipyard. Point Adams instructed Astoria Marine to install an eight-inch pipe from the lazarette to the engine room. The pipe was installed in order to house the hydraulic lines that ran from the engine room to the lazarette and passed through the vessel's crab tanks. Point Adams claims that, had this pipe been closed or capped, the water would not have passed through from the lazarette into the engine room.

Two points are of interest in the court findings:
1. The boat had sunk by flooding beginning in the lazarette, and

2. the statement added to the contract that the vessel had to be built to "the best commercial marine practice."

In retrospect, the delivery crew experienced major problems with the new *Scottie*. Many systems failed during the stormy voyage from Mobile to the Panama Canal. We thought that the complete flooding of the lazarette was due to improper securing of its deck hatch, but we did not actually check the seal. It could have been that, even when properly secured, the hatch did not seal and allowed seawater to flood into the lazarette. (Further research found that a number of king crab boats had water leaking into the lazarette through the shaft alley from their adjacent live tanks.) No high-water-level alarm had been installed in *Scottie*'s lazarette when we took delivery, or it would have sounded when the compartment flooded during the storm. With both live tanks filled and the flooding of the lazarette, we were lucky that the boat did not founder in the early hours of January 6, 1970.

When Astoria Marine installed an 8-inch open-ended pipe through the upper side of the live tanks as a conduit for critical hydraulic lines, it is likely that no one was aware that they may have been tapping into a fundamental

Seattle Daily Times (published as The Seattle Times) -
September 12, 1973 - page 50
September 12, 19: | Seattle Daily Times (published as The Seattle ˙ | Seattle, Washingtc | Page 5(

Maritime

Crab boat sinks; four men rescued

Times news services

Four fishermen were rescued from their liferaft in the Bering Sea yesterday after their 83-foot crab boat, the Scottie, began taking on water 16 miles northwest of Port Moller.

The Coast Guard said the Scottie issued a mayday call, reporting that water had gushed into the engineroom, causing the boat to sink quickly.

The crew abandoned ship and was picked up by the fishing vessel Sea Spray. The cutter Jarvis and two Coast Guard aircraft were sent from Cold Bay.

The skipper of the Sea Spray was identified tentatively as August Gudjonson.

The Coast Guard in Juneau said today the four rescued men were still aboard the Sea Spray. Officials were awaiting its arrival in port to learn what had caused the sinking.

News story about the sinking of the *Scottie*

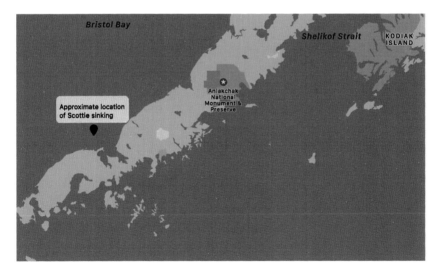

Map showing approximate location of the loss of the *Scottie*.

flaw of lazarette flooding in the vessel. The fact that the hydraulic steering lines had been run through the bottom of the crab tanks, which were filled with tons of seawater and live king crab when fishing, indicated that the *Scottie* was not built to best marine practices. This language was added to the original contract because Point Adams was concerned from the outset that Bender had minimal experience in building vessels to "best commercial marine practice" that could withstand winter fishing in the Bering Sea.

Any new vessel has a breaking-in period, which is why testing all systems on sea trials is a critical step in its acceptance. The *Scottie* did not undergo thorough sea trials. The subsequent system failures, however, pointed to deep problems with build quality, evidenced by the exposure of the critical hydraulic steering lines through the bottom of the two live tanks.

Scottie and *Stevie* were built in a hurry to get into the lucrative Alaskan king crab rush. Perhaps the more prudent approach would have been to order vessels from a Pacific Northwest yard which was building to higher quality for one of the toughest fisheries in the world. But were the owners' decisions out of the ordinary for that time? The 1965-66 king crab harvest, centered then in Kodiak, produced 94.4 million pounds with a value of $22 million. Individuals and fishing companies were rushing to get at this marine gold mine.

"It was like a fever sweeping the docks," remembered Bud Ryan, then a young Anacortes crabber as he stated in Patrick Dillon's *Lost at Sea*. (Bud Ryan and I graduated in 1966 from Anacortes High School.)

The *Scottie* could have been lost and us with her on at least two occasions during our delivery voyage. The residing irony lay in our "illusion" of an easy cruise through the Caribbean turning nearly deadly. The lessons learned about preparedness for a voyage and the indiscriminate power of the sea provided experience applicable to many of life's subsequent endeavors.

Point Adams lost its appeal against Astoria Marine and Bender in the case of the loss of the *Scottie*.

BIBLIOGRAPHY

Herman Melville, *Moby Dick,* Könemann Verlagsgesellschaft mbH, 1995 (originally published in Britain, 1851).

Joseph Conrad, *Youth*, Doubleday Page & Co., 1902.

Sebastian Junger, *The Perfect Storm,* W. W. Norton & Company, 1997.

Patrick Dillon, *Lost at Sea,* The Dial Press, 1998.

Redmond O'Hanlon, *Trawler,* Vintage Departures, 2003.

Dean J. Adams, *Four Thousand Hooks: A True Story of Fishing and Coming of Age on the High Seas of Alaska*, University of Washington Press, 2013.

Matt Lewis, *Last Man Off,* Plume Penguin Group, 2014.

ACKNOWLEDGEMENTS

Thanks to Ross Fearey, "Ah, the good old days."

To Kathleen Kaska, who provided invaluable direction in navigating the labyrinth to publishing and warned me that writing was the hardest thing she ever did. She retired from middle school science teaching.

To my family for giving me the time to write.

To Wendy and Mac, master proofreaders.

ABOUT THE AUTHOR

S tephen D. Orsini was born in Fairbanks, Alaska. As a young boy, he lived with his mother and three siblings in a small house on Guemes Island, in the San Juan Islands archipelago of Washington State. Stephen attended the first three grades in the island's two-room schoolhouse, then traveled daily by ferry to school in Anacortes, Washington. His attraction to adventure, writing, and the sea fused during his high school years, when he discovered the complete works of Joseph Conrad in the Anacortes Carnegie Public Library. Conrad's novelette *Youth* became the basis—years later—for his personal account of the delivery of the ill-fated new king crab vessel, *Scottie*.

Having grown up alongside the long Anacortes tradition of commercial salmon fishing, Stephen spent college summers commercial purse seining in the Alaskan waters of Southeast and Kodiak Island. In 1970 he graduated from Lewis and Clark College with a degree in English literature, after which he entered the Peace Corps and worked on a fisheries development program on the north coast of Honduras.

To support not only his family but also his addiction to sailing, Stephen spent 30 years in the power generation industry, marketing for major international firms. He has published freelance articles in the *National Fisherman, Oceans, The Compass, Sailing, Sailing World, 48 North, Private Pilot*, and *Highlights*, the magazine of the Camden Conference. He saved the delivery voyage of the *Scottie* for his first book.